AIRCRAFT ARMAMENT

Merle Olmsted

New York

MODERN AIRCRAFT SERIES
A Division of Sports Car Press

Library of Congress Catalog Card Number: 79-129095
ISBN 0-87112-033-X
©1970 by Sports Car Press, Ltd. and simultaneously in Ontario, Canada by General Publishing Company
Manufactured in the United States of America by Semline, Incorporated
All Rights reserved under International and Pan American Copyright Conventions

MODERN AIRCRAFT SERIES

Edited by Joe Christy

A new series of popular-priced books on aircraft and their operation for everyone interested in privately owned planes. Each volume is written by an expert in the field, and is printed on fine, white paper and profusely illustrated with photographs and diagrams. Each volume $2.95.

The Single-Engine Beechcrafts	Your FAA Flight Exam
Parachuting for Sport	Racing Planes Guide
Guide to Antique Planes	Lightplane Engine Guide
Cockpit Navigation Guide	The Piper Cub Story
Used Plane Buying Guide	Aircraft Dope & Fabric
Air Traffic Control	Agricultural Aviation
Modern Aerobatics	Your Pilot's License
Classic Biplanes	Instrument Flying Guide
Classic Military Biplanes	Soaring Guide
Aircraft Armament	Classic Monoplanes
Pilot's Weather Guide	Your Jet Pilot Rating
Computer Guide	Lightplane Construction & Repair
Club Flying	Taking Pictures From The Air
Guide to Homebuilts	Multiengine Flying
Fighter Aircraft Pocketbook	Airmanship After Solo
All About Helicopters	Legal Guide for Pilots & Owners

SPORTS CAR PRESS

Distributed by CROWN PUBLISHERS

419 Park Avenue South, New York, N.Y. 10016

ACKNOWLEDGEMENTS

This book was made possible by the co-operation of many people and organizations, and all are due my gratitude. Prominent among these are aviation writers Page Shamburger and Joe Christy. Major Jack Elliott and WO W. T. Heath, both retired from the Marine Corps, were generous with their help, as was Rowland Gill, USMC Historian.

The Public Relations officers of the Boeing Company, Bell Helicopter, Sikorsky, and Fort Rucker supplied much material, as did the Air Force Museum.

Lastly, my special thanks to Raymond Pritchard, old friend and intrepid air gunner of long ago!

Merle Olmsted

CONTENTS

		Page
	Introduction	7
I	Early Years and World War One	9
II	The Twenties and Thirties	37
III	Fighters of World War Two	45
IV	Bombers of World War Two	67
V	The Armed Chopper	91
VI	Fighters Since World War Two	99
VII	Vietnam	107

Cover Picture:
Air Force crew chief tests guns of Douglas A-26 (B-26 after 1947).
by *USAF*

INTRODUCTION

With the invention of the airplane was to come one of the greatest causes of change in history. Although probably no one realized it for a long time after man first soared into the air, the flying machine was eventually to change everything — for both good and bad. Its affect would be tremendous and was to be felt in some way or another by most of the civilized world and for much of the not so civilized. It would, in a short span of time, lead man to the moon.

Long before the Wrights produced the first practical flying machine man had been seeking more efficient ways to kill his fellow man. Why this trait, which dates to the very dawn of time, should be part of mans makeup is beyond this authors knowledge, and the scope of this book.

Although he again did not realize it at first, man was to find in the airplane, besides its great ability to improve his way of life, an equal ability to provide more efficient methods of making war.

Although the worlds military services of by-gone days have been roundly critized by those with hindsight, for not recognizing the potentialities of the airplane, there were few men of those times who could visualize the fantastic changes the flying machine would bring, or in fact, the giant advances that would be made in the machine itself in such a few short years.

It is true that to most military staffs of the worlds armies, the airplane was seen (if at all) as an extension of mans earthbound eyes. For at least two centuries in the western world the cavalryman had been the long range eyes of the military leaders. Without the horse soldiers to scout the enemy to determine his strength and weakness, his disposition and his plans, those who planned the battles of those years would have been totally blind.

When they did take note of the airplanes arrival on the scene early in this century, it was obvious to some of them that here was a considerable improvement on the horse soldier in some respects. The airborne scout could see more in less time, and travel far faster then the cavalryman. So it was that as heavier-then-air-machines began to join the world armies in the first decade of this century, their sole duty was thought to be reconnaissance.

The written records and those of the various patent offices indicate that many men, both airmen and those who had never seen an airplane, were aware of the advantage one flying soldier could have over another if he could carry a weapon aloft with him. There were, however, serious problems for these idea men, the most formidable being that the flying machine was barely able to stagger into the air with a pilot and maybe a passenger. If the overzealous crew were to add much in the way of armament, the machine would likely refuse to fly at all. In addition, those who were eager to try it, and finally did when the machines performance had improved a bit, were mostly the junior officers — enthusiastic, but with little rank to make themselves heard.

This book will attempt to chronicle the story, over considerably more than half a century, of the efforts to provide effective armament for military aircraft.

Any study of such equipment is interwoven with the story of the men, the designs, the manufacture, and the operation of the aircraft themselves. It would be impossible to separate the two narratives.

No attempt will be made however, to cover the subject of bombs or air-to-surface missiles.

I
EARLY YEARS AND WORLD WAR ONE

Much of man's history is lost forever, never recorded, or if it was it now often reposes in such obscure places as to never be found by the historian. For this reason it would be folly to try to identify, for sure, the first man to discharge a firearm from a heavier than air flying machine in flight.

In the United States, however, the record is fairly clear. The distinction goes to Lt. Jacob E. Fickle, U. S. Army. Fickle was not a flyer, but an officer of the 29th Regiment of Infantry. On the 20th of August, 1910, armed with a U. S. service rifle, a model 1903 Springfield, Fickle fired two shots into a ground target from an altitude of about 100 feet. The pilot for this early aerial gunner was the well known pioneer, Glenn Curtiss himself, and the location was the Sheepshead Bay Racetrack near New York City. Fickle had no turret, gunners cockpit, safety belt, or even a seat. He sat on the leading edge of the lower wing, to the left of Curtiss and fired his '03 downward through a maze of struts and wires.

The experiment proved little, of course, except that Fickle had a good sense of balance and was a rather good shot with the service rifle.

It would be almost two years before anyone in the United States was to try it with the weapon that would ultimately convert the airplane into a fighting vehicle — the machine gun.

College Park, Maryland was the first of the army aviation "schools." It was here, in the fall of 1909 that Lts. Frank Lahm and Frederic Humphreys soloed after training by Wilbur Wright and became the U. S. Armys' first HTA pilots.

Maryland's wintery weather was too severe for these early military aircraft, and early in 1910 the army moved its only airplane to the sunnier climes of south Texas. However, by the spring of 1912, College Park was again an active army flying center, and in June of that year Colonel Isaac Newton Lewis, U. S. Army Coast Artillery (retired), arrived at College Park to demonstrate his new machine gun to the flyers. Lewis is a name we will hear more of later, but at this time he was associated with the Automatic Arms Company of Buffalo, New York. Two years before, in 1910, he had agreed to assist that company in the development of a machine gun based on the patents of one Samuel Neal McClean.

By 1911, Lewis had completed the prototype of the famous Lewis gun, and along with four other hand made weapons, had been demonstrating them to various army agencies. It was in the course of these demonstrations that Lewis brought his guns to College Park.

These automatic weapons were not aircraft guns in any respect (there was in fact, no such thing), but they happened to be well suited for the purpose. They weighed only about 25 pounds and were quite easy to handle. They were air cooled. Since the gun was fed from a circular magazine there was no problem with flapping belts entangling the gunner or parts of the aircraft.

As can be imagined, the Lewis guns caused considerable interest at College Park, and Captain Charles Chandler was the man who first carried a Lewis aloft in a Wright Model B.

Lt. Thomas DeW. Milling was the pilot and Chandler sat next to Milling with the gun resting on his knees and the muzzle resting on a cross bar. The first flight was on the 7th of June, 1912. Chandler had not planned on firing the weapon the first flight, but only on finding the best position. However, finding that there was no problem, Chandler decided to go ahead with the firing trial.

The target was a piece of canvas about two feet square and Chandler was able to get about 12% of his burst into the target from some 300 feet altitude. Chandler had never fired a Lewis gun before this, and in addition he did not allow for the forward speed of the Wright B. The result was that most of the bullets struck ahead of the target.

The next day, the same crew tried again, this time from about 500 feet, with a 7′ x 6′ target. This time Chandler fired almost a full magazine (44 rounds) and got 14 hits on the target.

Eager to continue the trials, a request was made through the Chief Signal Officer to purchase ten Lewis guns. The request was passed to the Chief of Ordnance who turned it down since the Lewis was not an issue weapon, and none were to be had. He offered instead the standard army machine gun, the Benet Mercie, a gun de-

The first armed U. S. military airplane, a Wright B, at College Park, Maryland. The gunner (left) is Captain Charles DeF. Chandler who airfired this Lewis gun for the first time on 7 June 1912. The pilot in this photo is Lt. Roy Kirkland, but Lt. DeWitt Milling was pilot during the actual test. *Air Force Photo*

signed and built by the French Hotchkiss organization. Whether these were ever tried is not known, but the flyers did not find the gun satisfactory for airplane use and the matter was dropped.

Colonel Lewis took his four handmade machine guns and went to Europe soon after this, where, as we shall see, he fared consider-

Captain Chandler with the prototype Lewis machine gun, photographed at College Park in May 1912. Air Force Photo

ably better.

Although the Benet Mercie was not considered suitable by U. S. flyers, a similar machine gun had been fitted to a Deperdussin monoplane in France the same year (1912) that Chandler had first fired the Lewis from the air. While the latter had been carried in Chandlers lap, the French attempt included a raised railing around the front (gunners) cockpit, on which the gun was mounted. In order to use his weapon the gunner was required to stand up in the cockpit. Although apparently fragile and unsatisfactory, this was the origin of the gun ring which would be used for many years to mount flexible machine guns on multi-seat aircraft.

In the few years before World War One, all of the major automatic weapons and associated equipment that would be used in that war were either in existance or under development. All of the machine guns which would play major roles as aircraft armament were in existance, but not in their final aircraft form.

Although many different airborne weapons would be used in the First World War, only two basic types were of great importance, both from a quality and quantity standpoint. Strangely enough, both of these were the products of American arms designers.

One of these, Colonel Isaac Newton Lewis, has already been mentioned in connection with his demonstration at College Park in 1912. When he failed to stir up any interest or orders from the U. S. military services, he took his guns to Europe, and there in 1913 found immediate backing in a centuries old city of arms manufacturing — Liege, Belgium. There he formed a company to manufacture the Lewis machine gun. America, behind a vast bastion of water, saw little need for any extensive arms buying. In Europe, however, it was plain that a great storm was approaching.

British sources were also highly impressed with the Lewis and Birmingham Small Arms soon made arrangements to build the gun in England. Since the German army was to occupy Liege in only a few months, it was a fortunate arrangement.

When World War One began, the British army standard machine gun was the Vickers modified Maxim (discussed later), but nothing like the quantities needed could be obtained, so Lewis finally saw his gun go into mass production for the British army. By war's end BSA had built over 145,000 Lewis machine guns.

The Lewis was actually a light machine gun. Not normally equipped with a tripod mount, but with only two short support legs (a bipod) near the nuzzle. It was a gas operated weapon and fed from a circular magazine holding 47 rounds mounted on top of the gun. Its barrel was covered with a finned aluminum casting which in turn had a circular casing which extended slightly beyond the muzzle. When the gun fired, a low pressure area was created causing a cooling air flow from the rear of the barrel casing. This cooling arrangement was often removed and the gun worked as well, a point that would be of interest when the Lewis was remodeled as an aircraft gun.

The only other machine gun that would be of any importance in aircraft armament was the Maxim. Developed by another American, Hiram S. Maxim, it was to be, for over two decades, the most widely used machine weapon in the world.

Maxim was born in Maine in 1840 and from age 14 worked at many mechanical jobs, finally becoming in the 1880's, a very successful engineer in the infant electrical business. While in Europe on business in the early 1880's, he became aware of the intense interest in a new type of gun — the fully automatic weapon, or machine gun.

Although he had no knowledge of arms design, his fertile mind became interested in the problem and in 1884 he received his first British patent for a recoil-operated machine gun. The gun that Maxim developed to his patent ideas was to vary only in detail from guns made many years later.

The Maxim was an entirely different concept than the Lewis, being designed to be fired from a tripod, and falling in the later category of a heavy machine gun. It was belt fed and water cooled via a water jacket surrounding its barrel.

Maxim soon became associated with Albert Vickers Steel Company of Crayford, Kent, who were to manufacture his guns for many years. After the Maxim patents ran out Vickers was to continue manufacture of a modified version under its own name.

Ironically enough, this invention of an American, developed in England, was to greatly impress the military authorities of other nations, and early in the new century the German government began to build the Maxim gun at their Spandau Arsenal. When World War One burst forth, the German army had far more machine guns then any of its opponents, and the Maxim was its only major machine weapon throughout the years of that conflict.

In France, the clip-fed Hotchkiss light machine gun was coming into use in the French army, and would be used, in a small way, as an aircraft gun.

None of these, that summer of 1914, were considered as armament for the fragile airplane. Not yet, but soon.

The Great War of 1914-18 started with two shots from a Browning pistol, fired by a student with revolutionary ideas, in the city of Serajevo, in the Austrian province of Bosnia. The day was June 28th, 1914, and the victims were the Austrian Crown Prince, Franz Ferdinand, and his commoner wife. The tangled web of political intrigue, policies and complicated treaties had long since pushed the nations of the Balkan Peninsula on the downhill road to war. Serajevo was the latch on the trapdoor, and one by one the nations of Western Europe were dragged into the bottomless hole. The incredible slaughter of World War One would drag on for over four years.

It was primarily a ground war. Millions of men struggled, and died, for small bits of muddy land across the landscape of France in one of histories most costly wars.

By 1914 the major European nations were busily building up their air forces, as all of their military services. Although all of these air forces were ill-equipped and insignificant, they were far beyond anything imagined in the birthplace of the airplane — the United States. None of these European nations considered their "airpower" as a major force. In this they were quite correct, the air forces never were a decisive force in WW-I, although they did increase in importance far beyond that visualized in 1914.

None of the armies of Europe had any clear idea of what to do with their small forces of frail flying machines. It was recognized that they might prove useful for reconnaisance, but for little else. Since no form of combat was envisioned, no armament was provided for the machines of that era.

Hardly anyone knew, or cared, that the first aerial combat had already taken place the year before. This combat is said to have taken place in Mexico between two American flyers employed by opposing sides in one of the periodic Mexican revolutions. Late in 1913 Dean Lamb and Phil Rader exchanged pistol shots, with no decisive results. It is unlikely they were trying very hard, and the combat (if it happened) while interesting, is of no historic importance.

Even though the leaders of the warring powers considered the airplane as a non-combat type, the flyers, themselves had already figured out that a machine gun could be an important weapon if they could induce their underpowered craft to lift one into the air. The Great War was only a few days old before it was tried.

About a week after the declaration of war, the Royal Flying Corps (RFC) deployed most of its strength to France. It was a motley collection of flying machines that crossed the English Channel in mid-August, and included Bleriots, B.E.2s, Henri Farmans, and Avros. There were less then 40 of them, mixed indiscriminately, and they formed the equipment of #2 and #3 Squadrons and part of #4. Together they formed a large chunk of the RFCs total strength. None were armed with anything except possibly a British service rifle.

Among the aircrews of these squadrons was Lt. Louis A. Strange who was to have several hair raising adventures, but was destined to survive the war. His observer-about-to-become-gunner, was Lt. L. Penn-Gaskell, and the two of them had rigged an infantry type Lewis gun in the forward cockpit of their pusher Henri Farman.

On the 22nd of August they had their big chance when a German reconnaisance aircraft appeared over Mauberge Airdrome. The intrepid Britishers took off and gave chase in their Henri Farman. However, success was not to be theirs. When the Farman had reached its maximum altitude of about 3,500 feet the enemy aircraft was still far above and out of range of Penn-Gaskell's shiny new Lewis. Upon landing the useless gun was ordered removed, and to someone else would go the credit for the first successful use of an airborne machine gun.

During the early part of the war when the machine gun could not be carried because of the weight penalty on aircraft performance, many crews armed themselves with rifles, shotguns and pistols. There was little chance of success with them, but it has been claimed that R. J. F. Barton of the RFC, and Felix Brocard of the French Air Service both shot down German machines with pistol fire at close range.

Other more imaginative methods were also tried, including the throwing of bricks and hand grenades, and trailing a hook or heavy ball on a long cable from one's aircraft. The idea here, of course, was to damage the enemy machine by striking its propeller or other vulnerable part.

There seems little doubt that the credit for the first successful combat between machine-gun-armed aircraft, resulting in the destruction of one of them, goes to two French non-commissioned officers (NCOs). They were Sergeant Joseph Frantz, pilot, and Corporal Quenault (first name unknown), gunner.

Frantz was an unusual pilot in the fall of 1914, in that he already had six years of flying experience, having learned to fly in 1908. When he was inducted into the French army in 1912, he was assigned as a military pilot. When war began two years later he was with Squadron VB-24 (The VB stood for Voisin Bomber, the unit's aircraft equipment).

The pusher Voisins remained unarmed until late in August when Gabriel Voisin, the aircraft manufacturer, arrived at VB-24's home field with six Hotchkiss machine guns, some crude mounts, and the necessary 8 m/m ammunition. Gabriel Voisin had the desire to mate the guns with the bombers but would VB-24 co-operate? There was probably no lack of eagerness to do so. VB-24's mission was the usual reconnaisance of those early days, and included bombing missions against enemy troops using ten and twenty pound bombs which were tossed overboard by hand.

Frantz was returning from one of these missions on the 5th of October, 1914 when he became involved in a deadly serious battle with a two-seat German aircraft.

Frantz was not alone. He was flying the Voisin from the front cockpit with Corporal Quenault in the rear seat and one of the Hotchkiss guns in front of him on a post mount.

As soon as they spotted the approaching aircraft, both agreed that it was "Boche", and identified it as an Aviatik. Frantz held the height advantage and immediately dived to the attack. Converting his altitude into speed, the Voisin soon overtook the German aircraft which took immediate evasive action, the observer opening fire at the Frenchmen. Quenault returned the fire with his Hotchkiss.

The crews of VB-24 had already found that the Hotchkiss was not a very reliable weapon, stoppages being quite common. Another disadvantage of this gun for air use was that it was loaded with 24-round rigid strips. These ammo strips protruded from the right side of the weapon, and because of their small capacity required frequent replacement if much firing was done. Regardless of the faults, Quenault manned his gun like a professional, snapping out short bursts at the Aviatik.

The battle lasted several minutes, swirling lower until both aircraft were down to about 200 meters. By now Quenault had fired one clip and most of another — his last, when the Hotchkiss jammed.

As the gunner struggled with the gun in an attempt to clear it, the German aircraft rolled over on its back and dived into the ground.

The unfortunate German crewmen whose names appear not to have been recorded, died in the crash.

Sergeant Frantz is often credited with this first victory because he was the pilot, entirely ignoring the man who did the shooting. However, to these two French NCOs must go equal recognition as victors in the very first dogfight between machine-gun-equipped fighting aircraft.

With the coming of slightly more powerful engines and improved airplanes, the installation of guns became more common as the war moved into 1915, with more machines being armed, although often very crudely. The weapons on the Allied side remained the Hotchkiss and the ground-type Lewis. The former was not a successful airborne gun, and the French soon began to use the Lewis as their flexible weapon.

As was usual throughout the first three years of the war, the Germans held a technological lead over the Allies in most things aeronautical. Since Germany was the aggressor in WW-I, as in WW-II, it is natural that it would have expended far greater effort in all things military then the opposing side.

The pusher type aircraft was, in those early years, the most plentiful in the British and French service, and their first efforts at arming their flying machines mounted the gun on a swivel in the forward (sometimes the rear) cockpit, occupied by the gunner who had a wide free field of fire forward, and none whatsoever to the rear.

The tractor type aircraft was rapidly coming to the fore as the machine of the future. The tractor type is one in which the engine and propeller are mounted at the front of the fuselage, the thrust of the prop in a sense, pulling the machine through the air.

In almost all cases the tractor type was faster then the pusher and it was obvious that a fixed gun mounted on the fuselage and firing directly forward would have great advantages. The problem was to develop a means of doing so without hitting ones own propeller blades.

Strangely enough, the means to do so had been known for some time. These devices were to be known as synchronizers and one of the earliest seems to be that patented by Franz Schneider, an engineer working in Germany (although he is sometimes said to be Swiss). His patent for a synchronizer for a machine gun was granted in 1913.

These early machine gun-to-engine synchronizers consisted of a linkage between the engine and the firing mechanism of the gun, in which the engine actually fired the gun, timed to do so when the propeller was clear of the gun muzzle.

A variation of this, seldom used, was the interrupter gear, in which case the gun fired normally, in full automatic, but the engine linkage stopped the firing when propeller and gun were in line.

The Schneider arrangement seems to have been little used by the Germans although it was similar to later designs. By the time they were sufficiently interested to take action, it was the result of a crude French expedient which acheived successful fire through the propeller arc.

The series of incidents which jolted the Germans into action involved the destruction of several of their two-seat observation aircraft in the spring of 1915. These machines were shot out of the sky in a spectacular manner by a French pilot named Roland Garros, flying a single seat Morane Scout on which was mounted a Hotchkiss infantry machine gun (the same type used by Corporal Quenault six months before).

Garros was a famous pre-war flyer and when war came and he entered the French Air Service, he was assigned to Escadrille M.S. 23. Who orginated the idea of fitting steel deflector plates to the propeller, and letting the gun fire full automatic is not known. Garros was no doubt involved as was a man named Eugene Gilbert who is said to have tried it previously. The installation of the triangular plates and the gun was probably done at the Morane factory, and Garros took the contraption into combat for the first time about the 1st of April, 1915, when he shot down an Albatross crewed by Lts. Hugo Ackner and Fritz Dietrichs. Both German crewmen died, the victims of Garros' Hotchkiss.

No source seems to be clear on how many aircraft Garros shot down, but it was probably only three or four before he experienced engine failure on a bombing mission over Courtrai on the 19th of April, and landed the Morane reasonably intact. His attempts to burn it were unsuccessful before capture and the secret was out.

German airmen and technicians examined the "system" with considerable interest and called in Anthony Fokker to see it also. Fokker, although a Dutch citizen, was a famous pre-war flyer and fairly prominent aircraft builder in Germany, one of whose products was a single-seat mid-wing scout bearing a striking resemblance to the Morane Saulnier. This may have been the reason that Fokker was invited to come up with something similar. The Fokker E-1 (*Eindecker* — one wing, or monoplane), along with the Morane, were the closest to being what would later be called a fighter.

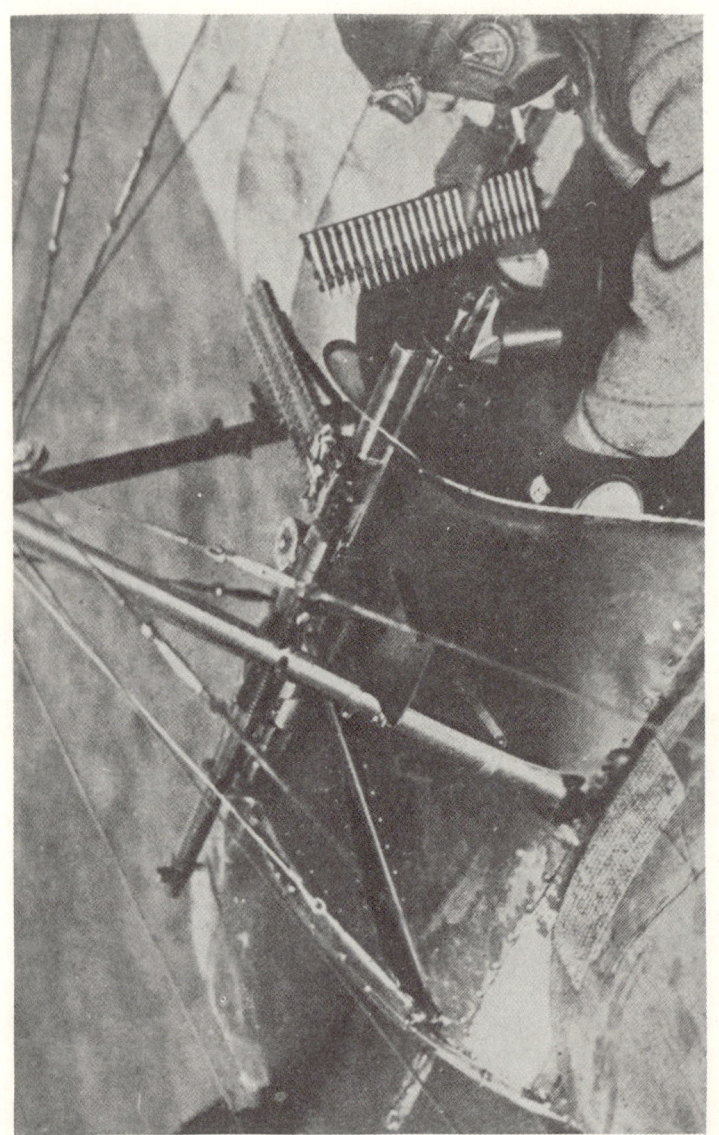

French Morane Scout with a Hotchkiss gun and steel deflectors on the prop blades. This may be the Garros machine. Joe Christy photo

The story of the development of the Fokker synchronizer gear is somewhat cloudy. Fokker, in his book *Flying Dutchman* published in 1931, claims sole credit for inventing the synchronized machine gun. Although he gives no dates, he says a Parabellum gun (with which he was completely unfamiliar) was turned over to him on a Tuesday evening in Berlin, and he returned to his factory on the train, carrying the weapon "under his arm." He goes on to say that by Friday of the same week he had returned to Berlin towing the *Eindecker* (without wings we assume) behind his automobile. On the E-1 he mounted the Parabellum and his new synchronizer, which he successfully demonstrated to German army officials.

He makes no mention of any other individual involved in synchronizer development and most reference works over the years have re-recorded the event as he told it. However, more recent researchers doubt that he accomplished the design himself. Fokker was not an engineer and he did have a competent engineering staff. It is logical to assume that he utilized them in the design of the synchronizer gear, just as he did in the design of his aircraft.

Who actually designed the Fokker gear is probably of little importance. The mechanism itself was highly successful (although not 100% reliable) and was used by the thousands on German aircraft throughout the remainder of the war.

The legendary German pilots Max Immelmann and Oswald Boelcke both scored victories with Fokker E-1s in August 1915, and both went on to increase their scores to about eight by early 1916.

The use of the Fokker synchronizer and the Parabellum gun on a relatively small number of *Eindeckers* swung the pendulum of superiority to the Germans for the first time in the new air war. This lead was held throughout 1915 and well into 1916 before improved Allied machines ended the so-called "Fokker Scourge," briefly at least. Immelmann himself was killed on 18 June 1916, in combat with an FE2b of 25 Squadron, RFC, crewed by Lt. George McCubbin and Corporal J. H. Waller. Whether Waller shot him down or he was the victim of failure of his own synchronizer gear is not clear. In any case Immelmann died in the crash at about the same time the "Fokker Scourge" was coming to an end.

The Allied aircraft which outclassed the delicate *Eindecker* in mid-1916 were the British pusher types, the single seat DH-2, the two-seat FE2b and Vickers Gunbus. Although an ungainly beast, the Gunbus was the first military aircraft to be specifically designed to carry a machine gun. The FE2b was similar in layout, had two guns, and was a better fighting machine.

The best of the Allied types however, was the product of a prewar French builder, and was the first of the famous Nieuport Scouts, the Type II, or *Bebe* (Baby) Nieuport.

The Type II was a beautiful machine, a small single seat tractor biplane, it looked as a fighter should look, and for 1916 it was very good indeed.

Even at this late date, however, none of these Allied types had a synchronized gun, all mounted the drum-fed Lewis, the Nieuport's gun being on the top wing and firing over the arc of the propeller.

By now the Lewis gun had been modified to suit its new role as an aircraft weapon. Although there were variations among Lewis aircraft guns, the usual changes were as described in the U. S. Air Services *Handbook of Aircraft Armament,* dated August 1918: "It differs from the army type in that the radiator has been removed, and a spade grip is used instead of a regular butt stock, and it is fitted with a recoil check. The gun is fed from a magazine holding 97 rounds. The weight of the gun is 18 pounds, and the rate of fire 600 rounds per minute (RPM)."

The recoil check mentioned above was the attachment screwed to the muzzle. Its purpose was to reduce recoil. The armament section of the AEF found, however, that the recoil check had little effect either way, and it was often removed.

As mentioned previously, it is difficult to understand the long Allied delay in supplying synchronized guns to their fighting airmen. A synchronizer-equipped Fokker E-1 was not captured until April of 1916, but by that time several designs for these devices were in existance in Britain.

The first Allied single-seat scouts to appear with synchronized guns were the British Sopwith Pup, and the French Nieuport Type 17. The famed Layfette Escadrille began trading in its Type II's for the Type 17 in September 1916. Both the Pup and the new Nieuport were armed with a single Vickers gun in front of the cockpit.

To synchronize this gun the French had developed their own gear, which may or may not have been influenced by the Fokker gear. The first of these, the Type I, was adapted to rotary engines only and used on Nieuports. The later Type II was developed for the Spad, and it operated on a cam at the rear of the Hispano Suiza engine's cam shaft. Both were of the mechanical type, and both were

This U. S.-built DH-4 carries unusually heavy armament. Besides two synchronized Marlin guns and twin flexible Lewis guns, another Marlin is installed on the lower wing, apparently adjusted for ground strafing.
Air Force Photo

highly successful.

While the Fokker gear was mechanical, as was the French, using the engine through a rod linkage to fire the gun when the prop blades were clear of the muzzle, the most widely used British type was a hydraulic mechanism. Several British synchronizer designs appeared in 1915 and 1916, but none were produced in quanity until that designed by a Roumanian, living in England, George Constantinesco, entered service. This was the famous C.C. gear and it probably began to appear early in 1917.

The C.C. gear was not, however, the first British synchronizer. The Challenger, built by Vickers was used in small numbers on Sopwith 1½ Strutters. These aircraft were two-seaters and not scout or fighter types, although they were used in this role for want of something better.

Another British synchronizer was the Sopwith Kauper, which was a mechanical device like Fokkers', but its use was also limited.

The C.C. gear was to be the most successful and was, in fact, to remain standard on British fighters until well into the 1930s.

Nieuport 17's of the Lafayette Escadrille, taken on the Somme in 1916. Raoul Lufberry is seated in the cockpit, while Soubiran and Masson play with "Whiskey", one of the squadron's two lion cubs. Air Force Photo

There was no mechanical linkage in the C.C. gear, only a bowden cable from the pilots control stick to a needle valve at the bottom of an oil resevoir. Oil under pressure was piped to one side of a small plunger when the stick trigger was squeezed. The other side of the plunger rode on a camplate driven by the engine. When the rotating cam struck the plunger, it transmitted a hydraulic impulse through a pipe line to the trigger motor of the gun. Each time the rotating cam struck the plunger the gun fired.

The hydraulic synchronizers such as the C.C. gear also had their faults. The piping required close watching for leaks, and low oil pressure and air in the system were also common troubles. All could throw off the timing and result in holed or shattered propellers. All of these faults could be kept to a minimum by good maintenance, and with this gun gear, and the French mechanical devices, the Allies had solved one of their major armament problems.

By the time the Sopwith Pup and Nieuport 17 began to reach operational squadrons, the Germans were countering with the excellent Albatross machines with two synchronized guns — and so it went, the see saw technical battle for superiority. In the end the Allies would field a line of outstanding single and two seat aircraft which would take part in the defeat of an equally well equipped German Air Force.

The upper wing Lewis and cowl Vickers installation can be seen in this excellent photo of Dudley Hill and his Nieuport 17.   Air Force Photo

By the time the United States declared war on Germany in April, 1917 aircraft armament in Europe was just settling into the standards that would remain not only throughout the war, but for nearly two decades.

In the United States there was little knowledge of combat aircraft, or of machine guns for that matter. The British and French had been reluctant to supply information on their latest developments to a neutral U. S., and as a consequence, when President Wilson finally declared war the aviation scene in America was a sad one.

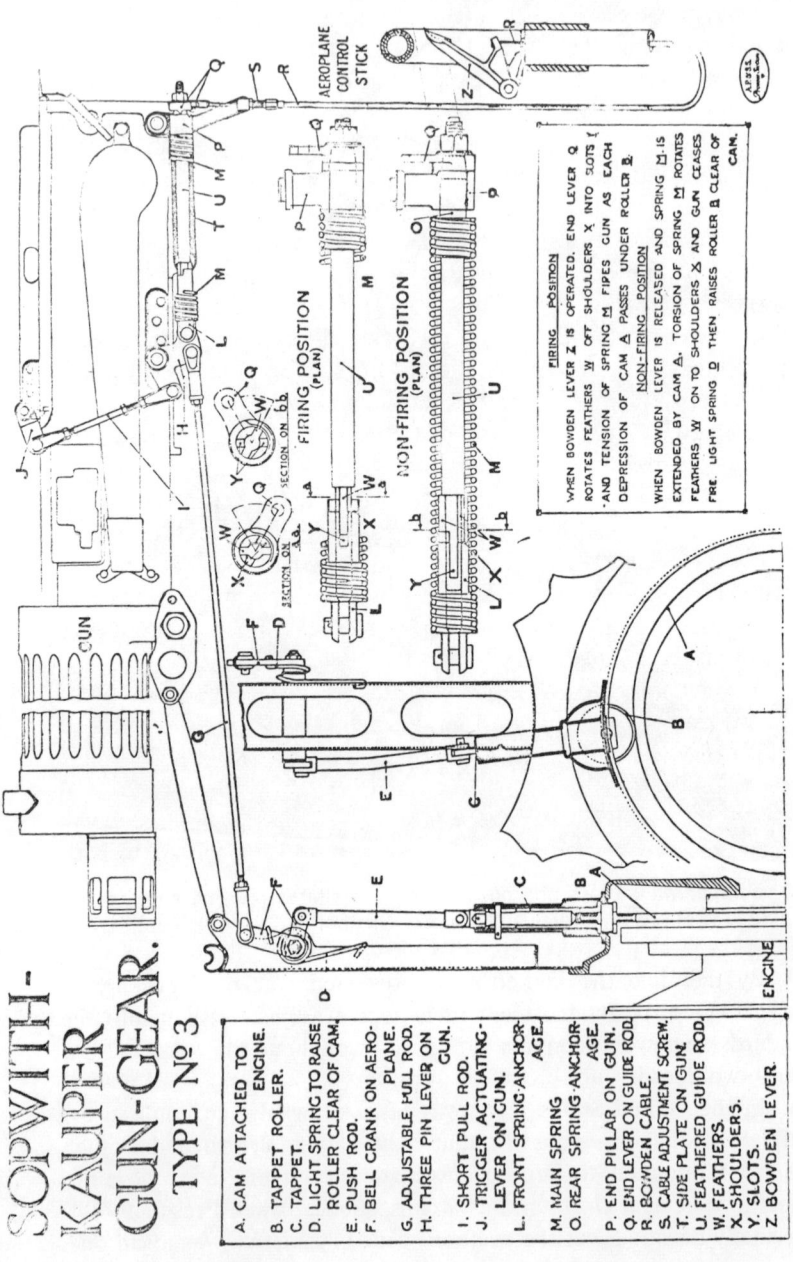

Although not as widely used as other synchronizer gears, the Sopwith Kauper type is typical of mechanical gun synchronizers.

Joe Christy Photo

The infant air arm of the U. S. Army had had all it could handle in the previous five years just acquiring aircraft suitable for flight, and there had been little thought of arming them. After Chandler had air tested the Lewis at College Park in 1912, there had been few developments in the airborne armament field.

The Army air arm in those pre-WW-I years was organized as part of the Signal Corps and late in 1914 the Chief Signal Officer received a suggestion from the Chief of Ordnance, that the Signal Corps might experiment with machine guns on aircraft. By that time these weapons had been carried aloft in the European war and used for offensive purposes. It had in fact, been more then a month since two unknown German flyers had died as the result of gunfire from Corporal Quenault's Hotchkiss, but it is unlikely that General Crozier, Chief of Ordnance, was aware of the incident.

As a result of this suggestion, two machine guns were shipped to the Signal Corps Aviation Center at North Island (San Diego).

One of these guns was a Vickers. Manufactured in the U. S. by the Colt Company, it was adopted as the Model 1904, but very few guns were purchased as a result of this adoption. The other gun was the Model 1909 Benet Mercie, which was basically a French Hotchkiss design. As far as can be discovered, neither gun was installed or tested at North Island.

At about this same time a Benet Mercie gun had been installed and flown on a newly delivered Burgess-Dunne armoured seaplane. This took place at College Park, but again it is not known if the weapon was ever fired.

Back at North Island, in the summer of 1914, there was considerable testing of small bombs and of the Riley Scott bombsight, but again this came to nothing.

Soon after the bombing tests in September, a new weapon of which we will hear more later, was inspected by Ordnance and Signal Corps officers. This was the Davis non-recoil 6 pounder airplane gun, manufactured by the New London Ship and Engine Company of Groton, Conn.

This unusual gun was the invention of Commander Cleland Davis, USN, and when he first applied for a patent in August 1911, there were few airplanes in existance which could even lift it. The gun was built in a ten foot tube open at both ends. When the 6 lb. projectile was fired through the forward end of the tube, the entire gun itself was blown out the rear end of the tube! Only one shot per flight could be fired and Davis soon had it redesigned so that a special shell could be loaded with the tube broken in its center. Now when it fired, the projectile went one direction and a charge of lead shot or metal filings of equal weight were blown out the aft end of the tube. The weapon could now be loaded in flight. The use envisioned by Davis for his gun was against water and ground targets such as ships and forts. It was not an air-to-air weapon, but would be one day. It was far too heavy and cumbersome and the army could see no use for it in 1914.

The raid of a Mexican bandit in March of 1916 was to involve the small U. S. air arm in its first actual field operation. On the 9th of that month, "Pancho" Villa crossed the Rio Grande and raided Columbus, New Mexico with a force upwards of 500 men. The interesting story of this raid, the most recent armed invasion of the United States, is beyond the scope of this book, but a few details are of interest as it led to the first use of the air arm.

What prompted Villa to undertake the raid can only be speculated upon, but he did succeed in burning much of the town and killing about 17 people, mostly civilians. To accomplish this Villa took heavy losses, as elements of the 13th Regiment of Cavalry were encamped in the town, and despite the surprise and confusion, troopers of the 13th managed to get to the guard tent and get four Benet Mercie machine guns into action. In an hour and a half they fired 20,000 rounds at the shadowy Mexicans silhouetted against the burning buildings.

As a result of this raid, General John "Blackjack" Pershing was ordered to the border to track down Villa and put an end to the border raids. He failed to acheive the first objective, but generally succeeded in the latter.

Ordered to join Pershing at Columbus was the Army's 1st Aero Squadron, then stationed at San Antonio.

No lengthy discussion of the expedition is required here because the 1st Aero was used mostly for scouting and courier duty — it did no fighting. Of interest however, is the fact that some sources say that among the equipment of the squadron were enough machine guns to arm all aircraft (eight Curtiss JN-3's), but no evidence has been found to show that guns were ever carried. Since the JN-3's were underpowered and totally unsuitable for the mission it is not difficult to see why.

In May, 1916, twelve Curtiss R-2s were received at Columbus

by the 1st Aero Squadron, and each was equipped with a Lewis gun, but these machines were no better then the JN-3's and the guns of no more use. These Lewis guns were almost surely in .303 British caliber, part of a batch of 350 the army had hurriedly bought from the Savage Arms Company for use by the Pershing Expedition.

As the spring of 1917 approached, America was about to become involved in an incredible war, the scope of which was far beyond anything imagined. Its tiny air arm was equipped with totally unsuitable aircraft, and its airmen had never fired a shot in anger — and very little in practice.

When President Wilson declared war on Germany on the 6th day of April, 1917, the United States military services had 55 airplanes. The NACA advised that 51 were obsolete, while the other four were slightly better, being merely obsolescent.

The overwhelming problems facing the military and industry of the United States cannot be covered here in any detail. Suffice to say that our exhausted allies, the British and French, particularly the latter, were making quite impossible demands for aircraft and crews — demands that were readily agreed to in this country.

The U. S. air effort has been roundly criticized ever since 1918, and there was a great deal of confusion and inefficiency. However, the achievements were also very great.

When the war ended only 19 months later, there were 45 American combat squadrons at the front in France. Production of airplanes had also been excellent considering the state of the industry in that spring of 1917 (slightly over 9500 training aircraft had been delivered by November 1918).

As is well known, the production of combat aircraft had not gone well, and all but a few of the 45 American squadrons flew only French and British aircraft. Aircraft armament used by the United States units in France was identical, for the most part, to their allies, and can be summed up in two words — Vickers and Lewis.

The Vickers, in production by Colt, had an excellent reputation, but it was a difficult weapon to produce and the demands for it far outstripped production. In order to release as many Vickers as possible for the foot soldiers of the machine-gun-starved American Expeditionary Force (AEF), the Marlin Rockwell Company of New Haven redesigned the old Colt-Browning "Potato Digger" for aircraft use. The swing-under lever was the major fault for aircraft use and this was replaced by a reciprocating gas piston in a housing beneath the barrel. The re-design was done in a few weeks and Marlin put the gun in production as the Model 1917. It weighed 22.5 pounds and had a rate of fire of 630 rounds per minute. Marlin built 23,000 of these, plus 15,000 of the slightly modified M1918. This was the first U. S. synchronized aircraft gun and remained in use only a few short years until replaced by the Browning.

Most sources say that no Marlins arrived in France until October, 1918, and none were used in combat. However, photos of the DH-4's of the 11th and 20th Squadrons of the 1st Day Bombardment Group in France, show clearly that Marlin guns were mounted on the cowls. In the Fall 1961 issue of *Cross and Cockade,* Clifford Allsopp, an observer with the 11th recalls that they were issued new U. S. built DH-4's with Marlin fixed guns in September, 1918.

An even more authoritative source, a lengthy report from the Chief Ordnance Officer of the AEF, indicates that these Marlin armed DH-4's were equipped with U. S. built C.C. synchronizing gear. This report also clearly shows that a considerable number of Marlins were also installed on Spad XIII's, but the guns had arrived with no synchronizing equipment at all, and they were adapted to use the French Type II mechanical gear.

Although the Marlins gave satisfactory service with the U. S. Service, the Vickers was preferred. It was much easier to maintain and was considered a very reliable weapon.

The first aircraft supplied to the Air Service of the AEF came from the French, and these were already armed with Vickers guns in .303 British caliber (which was also standard for that gun in French service). These .303 guns gave excellent service, but a changeover was begun to the standard .30-06 caliber Vickers as they became available in order to simplify ammunition supply problems. The .30-06 guns supplied by the AEF were ground guns and the Aircraft Armament Section had to do considerable modification to fit them for air use.

The change in caliber also required modifications in the aircraft themselves as the U. S. .30-06 cartridges were too long for the ammunition boxes which had to be re-designed.

In addition to the standard Vickers firing .303 British and .30-06 cartridges, there was an 11 m/m Vickers which saw limited services. Except for scaling up the necessary parts it was identical to the smaller weapon, and was designed to fire tracer and incendiary ammunition for attacks against observation balloons. The muzzle

Twin Vickers armament of a Spad 13, with Captain Edward Rickenbacker of the 94th Pursuit Squadron. Air Force Museum

velocity of the bullet was less then the calibers .30's, but was sufficient for use against the tethered balloons which could take little evasive action.

Although widely used by other countries, the Lewis never was considered a suitable ground machine gun by the U. S. Army and most Lewis guns built in the U. S. were the aircraft type, over 39,000 being built by the end of the war. They were used almost entirely as flexible guns in observers cockpits. The Lewis never was suitable for synchronizing.

Like the Vickers, the first Lewis guns received by the AEF were .303 British caliber obtained from the French. These gave excellent service but were later replaced by guns in standard U. S. caliber. The first of these later received by the Air Service were ground guns turned in by the Marine Corps. These were modified for aircraft use, where they gave a great deal of trouble as they would not function reliably with the gun in certain positions. This trouble was finally overcome by drilling out the gas ports in the barrel, allowing more powder gases to be applied to the head of the operating piston, thus increasing reliability to a high level.

Airmen had no sooner struggled into the blue with a rifle-caliber machine gun than they began to think even bigger: today a machine gun — tomorrow a cannon! Looking back through the technical literature and reports of the era, it is surprising how much effort was applied to the problem of making the shell firing gun into an aircraft weapon. Despite all of this effort there were no really successful airborne cannon installations until the late 1930s.

On the first day of October, 1918, the Interallied Aviation Committee issued a lengthy report on the use of cannon in aircraft. It refers to the use of a cannon mounted in a fixed position between the engine cylinder banks and firing through the hollow propeller shaft, and dismisses the idea as not seeming to "be a very good one." It recommends that the idea of installing a cannon in the engine should be completely given up. The remainder of the 20 page report is devoted to the coming use of flexibly-mounted cannon of 37 m/m for air to air combat, and "bombardment cannon" of 75 m/m to be used for ground attack in place of bombs.

With the advantage of hindsight it is interesting to see that both of the latter ideas were blind alleys leading nowhere, while the engine mounted cannon, so easily dismissed, was the only one of the three types to be used in large numbers in the years to come.

The 37 m/m engine cannon had, in fact, been used in combat in WW-I. This gun was developed at the French Puteaux Arsenal, and in many publications it has been described as "semi-automatic." However, the operation of the gun required that the pilot reload after each shot. This would make it a simple single shot weapon, not a semi-automatic. The latter type fires only one shot at a time, but does extract and eject the empty case, and reload the firing chamber, leaving it ready for the next shot. Another term for this type of gun is self loader.

The Arsenal produced 200 of these guns and they were installed between the cylinder banks of the 220 HP V8 Hispano engine in a single-seat Spad XII. This engine employed propeller reduction gearing, which placed the short hollow prop shaft higher then the engine crankshaft, and the cannon barrel was placed inside the prop shaft and fired through the prop hub.

About 30 of these aircraft were on the front at one time, and several of the best known French pilots such as Guynemer and Fonck are said to have scored victories in them. A single shot cannon was of limited use however, and after the first 50 guns with rifled barrels, they were issued with an interchangeable smooth bore barrel and cannister ammunition. In effect, this made them a huge shotgun, and did improve their effectiveness at short range. However, there was considerable trouble with the geared Hisso engine and pilots did not favor the single shot weapon. A full automatic version was developed at Puteaux Arsenal, but too late for WW-I. Twenty years later the engine cannon would be an important item in some air forces.

The flexibly mounted cannon never did develop into an important weapon, but heavy cannon up to 108 m/m, were installed in fixed mounts in multi-engine bombers in WW-II. Here again though, they were of limited importance.

By November, 1918, when a beaten Germany finally surrendered to equally exhausted Allies, aircraft armament was fairly well standardized among the warring powers.

Although, as discussed previously, a great deal of experimental work had been done on cannon by both the Germans and the Allies, none had been employed with much success in combat. Fighter type aircraft of the Royal Air Force, the French, German, Italian, and the U. S. air services were almost invariably armed with two rifle caliber machine guns, synchronized to fire through the propeller disc. Most carried an ammunition supply which would allow about 20 seconds firing time. The guns themselves were also very similar as we have seen. The Vickers used by all of the Allies, and the German Spandau and Parabellum, were all variations of the original Maxim gun.

There were exceptions to the rule, of course. On the Allied side, the wing mounted Lewis firing over the propeller was a relic of 1916, but it was used on the successful British S.E. 5, in conjunction with a single synchronized Vickers until the end of the war. The S.E. 5 Lewis was installed on a Foster mount, which allowed it to be pulled

This pristine S.E.5, bearing the zig zag markings of 40 Squadron RAF, was photographed in 1962, not 1918, but shows the Lewis gun and the optical Aldis sight to good effect.   Author's Photo

down and back on a curved rail. It could be fired at varying angles from near vertical to near line of flight.

The multi-seat combat aircraft showed less similarity. German bombers and two-seat observation aircraft were almost invariably armed with variations of the old Maxim in the form of the Parabellum 14, and the newer LMG 14/17. Although the Germans experimented with twin gun mounts for gunners, those in service were almost always mounted singly. Twin Parabellums were much more bulky and awkward than the comparable Lewis, which, incidently, was used for considerable experimental work by the Germans. The Parabellum type flexible guns were belt-fed weapons, the belt being wound on a circular feeder attached to the side of the gun and looking like a drum type magazine — which it was not.

In the Allied Services the standard flexibly mounted machine gun was the Lewis, modified for aircraft use, and equipped with a 97 round magazine. These were invariably mounted on a Scarff Ring in the observers or gunners cockpit, either singly or in pairs. Although two guns obviously provided double the fire power, there

The Armament Section of the 166th Aero Squadron, of the 1st Day Bombardment Group, in France in 1918. Lewis guns and one Marlin are visible.   Author's Photo

was also the disadvantage of added weight on the aircraft, resulting in decreased performance. It was tougher on the gunner also, who had more weight to swing against a powerful slipstream.

There was, of course, even in those primitive days, considerably more to an armament installation then the guns. Most of these would involve rather dull technical discussions and will not be gone into here except to mention some of the major components.

Ammunition containers were an important part of the installation, as were the necessary hoppers and chutes to collect the empty cartridge cases and the metal links of the disintegrating belts. These simple devices if not correctly designed and maintained, could cause interference with gun feeding, or the jamming of empty cases in the gun action, putting it out of commission.

Gun sights were also of considerable importance if the gunner was to hit his target. The British Aldis, an optical type, was very good, but had the problems of all optical sights — moisture fogging and being obscured by oil — especially severe with the castor oil lubricated rotary engines. The common ring and bead sight was the most widely used of all fixed gun sights. On flexible Lewis guns, the Norman wind vane sight was standard. This sight automatically compensated for the speed of the aircraft by the slipstream force applied to it. The main problem encountered with this sight was when firing directly aft. In this case the eddies of air current around the gunners

The Salmson 2A2 was widely used by Squadrons of the AEF, and this one, with its radial engine putting out plumes of smoke, is secured in a pit where its synchronized guns will be test fired. Instead of the usual single Vickers, this Salmson carries two fixed Marlin guns.

Page Shamburger Photo

body disturbed the sight. A fixed ring and bead was often mounted to be used in these situations.

Such was the armament and equipment of the fighting air forces in November of 1918 when the Great War finally ended with the collapse of the German nation.

II
THE TWENTIES AND THIRTIES

In the years after WW-I there was a minimum of development work on new aircraft armament. The momentum obtained during the war carried some experimental projects into the 1920s, but for the next twenty years anything that cost much money went by the boards. Germany was defeated and in political chaos, and little was to be done with the many advanced armament projects underway at the time of defeat, although many in the German arms trade moved to Switzerland to continue their work.

In the home countries of the victors there was no mood to spend money on any kind of armament. Germany was no longer a threat, and in 1919 it would have been difficult to make a case against any country as being a threat to peace. When that threat did materialize 20 years later, a large part of it would be the same old enemy, ready to try again.

In Britain the RAF of the 1920s was more like a small and happy group of flying club airmen. The better types of wartime aircraft remained in service well into the 1920s, and when they were replaced with new fighters and general purpose types, they had slightly improved performance and reliability over the 1918 counterparts, but retained the familiar layout and their offensive and defensive armament remained the same — the Lewis and Vickers. Since the aircraft had changed so little there was no need for any change in guns. What had been suitable for Camels and Spads remained suitable for Bristol Bulldogs and Fairey Flycatchers.

In the United States the situation was much the same. The two air arms, Navy and Army, shrank to insignificant levels and for almost twenty years the services spent — often unwisely — what little money was available on enough new aircraft, engines, and other equipment, to keep them going, but just barely. Throughout the 1920s there was but one single fighter group (the 1st Pursuit at Self-

A recoiless Davis gun mounted on a Curtiss HS-1 of the USN. The Lewis was used to "get on the target" before the Davis was fired.

Navy Department Photo

ridge Field) to defend the entire continental United States. There was also one bombardment group (the 2nd, at Langley Field), and one attack group (the 3rd, at various bases in the southwest). All were poorly equipped, undermanned and undertrained.

There were, however, a few developments in the aircraft armament field of those lean years. Beginning after WW-I and for 30 years thereafter, the only machine gun of any importance in the U. S. military services was the Browning. In addition to its dominance of the U. S. military scene, the Browning was used in vast numbers throughout the world and even today will be found in large numbers in the arsenals of the smaller countries, and still in limited use in the U. S.

These machine guns were the work of John M. Browning, an inventive genius who spent much of his life in the designing of sporting rifles, shotguns, and pistols.

Born in 1855 in the frontier city of Ogden, Utah, John M. followed in the family tradition as a gunsmith in an era and an area where the rifle was still an important tool for Mr. Average Man.

In 1889, he became interested in utilizing the energy of burning powder gases to operate the loading mechanism of magazine rifles, and converting them to semi or full automatic.

By 1890 he had progressed to a full fledged machine gun, which he offered to the Colt Company. Already well known in the arms trade, Browning's offer was accepted and, built by Colt, this gun became the Model 1895 and was used in small numbers by both the U. S. Navy and the Army, where it earned the nickname "Potato Digger" because of its swing underlever which operated the action. When WW-I began, the army possessed the insignificant number of 158 of the model 1895. Modified by Marlin, as already discussed, it became the Model 1917 and 1918 aircraft guns.

After the limited success of the Model 1895, Browning abandoned the gas operation principal and developed a recoil operated water-cooled machine gun which he patented in 1901.

For the next 17 years only sporadic development was done on the new gun because of a complete lack of U. S. military interest, and during this period Browning concentrated on sporting arms.

Early in 1917 the U. S. Army discovered, with considerable surprise it seems, that it would soon be expected to fight a very large war, and was lacking in everything required to do so.

At that time the machine gun was not an important weapon in the U. S. Army, although the fighting in Europe for the past three years should have indicated the need. A frantic call soon went out to arms designers, and in February, 1917 Browning took his machine gun (and his automatic rifle — the famous BAR) to Washington for demonstration to the Ordnance Department.

Although the performance of the machine gun was impressive, no action was taken until May when it was again tested and finally accepted (The BAR had been adopted after the February tests).

Of course by that time it was too late to put the gun into production, and phase enough into service for the AEF. Nevertheless, quite a few did reach France where they saw considerable action and performed remarkably well.

This machine gun, which became the Model 1917, was to be the basis for all Browning machine guns, with very little change, for the next 40 years. About 42,000 of the water cooled ground guns were built before the end of WW-I.

Almost immediately after introduction of the M1917, efforts were turned toward modifying it into an aircraft weapon.

The water cooling had to go, of course, as it was useless and unnecessary on an aircraft gun. (In later years it was also found to be unnecessary on the ground guns).

The machine gun that emerged as the Browning aircraft gun M1918, was developed through the M1918A1, M1919, M1921, and M1922. There was very little difference in any of them, the changes mostly having to do with reducing the weight of the operating parts to increase the rate of fire.

Only one Browning aircraft machine gun reached France during WW-I, and it was still in testing when the war ended.

The Browning was such an outstanding gun that there was no question of its not becoming standard in the U. S. services after the war. Although the Vickers and Lewis remained as limited standard and war reserve for many years, all U. S. military aircraft after WW-I were designed to be armed with the Browning. All of the various slight modifications were eventually consolidated in the aircraft gun M2 (later re-designated AN-M2). Its caliber was the usual .30-06, which it fired at about 1200 rounds per minute. It was arranged so it could be fed from either left or right side using the disintegrating link belt, and this weapon remained as the standard fixed and flexible machine gun until finally replaced by the caliber .50 early in WW-II.

There was one small step forward in the armament of U. S. combat aircraft soon after the great war, which would lead eventually to the excellent fighter weapon layout of 20 years later.

This small step was the designing of the airframe gun mount on the right side of U. S. pursuit aircraft so that a caliber .50 Browning M1921 could be installed in place of the usual caliber .30 gun. These were still the cowl-mounted synchronized guns of WW-I, but now a big .50 could be used, which had over twice the extreme range of the smaller gun (about 4,000 yards extreme effective range for the .50).

The .50 Browning was to be of tremendous importance in later years, but its origins go back to WW-I, soon after John Browning's M1917 had been accepted by the U. S. government.

Colonel John Parker, C. O. of the army machine gun school in France is said to have been the one who started the ball rolling on

The standard Army bomber in the decade of the 1920s was the Martin MB-2 series, seen here with twin Lewis guns in the rear cockpit, and the nose gunner manning a single Browning. Author's Photo

the .50. The French had developed an 11 m/m cartridge, primarily for use against balloons, which has been previously discussed. Parker was impressed with its possibilities and sent samples of the cartridge to the Ordnance Department in the U. S.

With unusual promptness Colt was ordered to build eight Brownings chambered for the French 11 m/m cartridge. However, before completion of the test guns, General Pershing himself had been heard from. Although he to was impressed by the idea, he felt the French cartridge had too little bullet weight and too little velocity.

As a result the test guns were taken to the Winchester Company where a new cartridge was designed along the lines of Pershing's ideas. The first gun was assembled and tested in September, 1918, but during firing it was found the big gun was difficult to handle and the ammunition was still not what was desired.

At this point the Germans unknowingly took a hand it its development. Captured examples of their much superior 13 m/m anti-tank cartridge were delivered to Winchester who then re-designed their own .50 caliber cartridge to give about the same ballistic performance as the German 13 m/m.

From this was born the caliber .50 Browning, too late for the 1914-18 war, but to be vitally important in the next one. The .50 Browning varied little from the smaller weapon, except for the scaling up of all parts and the addition of an oil buffer to handle the heavier recoil.

The big Browning saw little use in aircraft in the 1920s and 1930s, even though army pursuits were designed to mount one. The cost of ammunition played a big part in its sparse usage. For instance, the 8th Pursuit Group based at Langley Field, fired only 11,167 rounds of caliber .50 in practice for the training year 1935/36, but fired 303,000 rounds of caliber .30. At this time the 8th Group was flying a mixture of the standard pursuit aircraft of the era, the Boeing P-12 and the Curtiss P-6E.

During that same period the 2nd Bomb Group, also at Langley, fired only 247,177 rounds of caliber .30, and no caliber .50 since its bombers had only the smaller weapons. (Keystone B-6 bombers during the early part of the period, and Martin B-10s later). Gunnery tests of both units that same year showed very poor results.

The pattern was similar throughout the years of peace, gunnery training was always totally inadequate because ammunition was not available for a really comprehensive training program.

There appears also to have been a shortage of caliber .50 guns. The quarterly test of aircraft with full military load in 1933 was scheduled to be done on bombers "carrying one flexible aircraft machine gun, caliber .50 Browning, in the rear gunners cockpit for each 3rd bombardment airplane." The test was not carried out as planned as there were no flexible mounts for the .50 available, which was of little importance in any case, since there were no caliber .50 guns in stock either.

Four years later, in 1937, a report from the 2nd Wing of the GHQ Air Force at Langley Field stated "The present state of efficiency of flexible gunnery is worse then it was in 1918." This report, and many similar, indicate that the service was well aware of its deficiencies in aircraft armament training, but the sources of the shortages usually precluded any hope of correction by the services themselves.

U. S. Army and Navy fighters of those inter-war years require no lengthy discussion because the biplane Curtiss and Boeing pursuits remained standard until the mid 1930s and exhibited nothing new in their armament.

The Douglas O-2H was a standard observation type, and this one is seen at Langley Field in the late 1920s. The aircraft is part of the 12th Observation Squadron, and its gunner is swinging a single Lewis during annual gunnery competition. Author's Photo

The story is the same in regards to bombers and observation types. Photos of the period indicate that only rarely were the Lewis and Brownings removed from the armory and installed on the gun rings of the Martin, Curtiss, and Keystone bombers of those years. Only during the annual gunnery sessions were the guns to be seen.

Change began to occur in the mid 1930s, but even here, although the switchover to all-metal monoplanes was radical enough, the gun layout often remained the same!

In the United States, the development of aircraft cannon again began to receive attention in the early 1930s. About that time the American Armament Corporation began to work on a 37 m/m version. By that time the work being done in Europe on 20 and 25 m/m weapons was well known and the new gun was meant to counter these weapons, which it ultimately did not do. The 37 m/m gun was made in two versions, one for fixed mountings, and a lighter gun for power turret installation. As with earlier attempts at such installations, the turret gun was never utilized.

The fixed 37 m/m gun was used in the U. S. service only to a limited extent. The most important use of the 37 was in the Bell P-39 Airacobra which had a single such gun firing through the hollow prop shaft, although some models of the same aircraft had a 20 m/m in place of the 37.

Cannon of this caliber and above were found to fire too slow for air-to-air combat during WW-II, and the 20 m/m became the most widely used caliber. In the U. S. services, however, none of the shell firing guns approached the importance of the caliber .50 Browning.

III
FIGHTERS OF WORLD WAR TWO

As the inevitability of war became evident in Europe, the two nations that would become the major warring powers, Britain and Germany, were developing fighter and bomber armament that varied considerably.

In the Island Kingdom the biplane fighter with two .303 Vickers Mark II guns had plodded on into the 1930s by which time it was becoming amply clear that the concept was rapidly reaching the end of the line. Nevertheless, there were many in the military

U. S. WW-II FIGHTER ARMAMENT

TYPE ACFT	DESIGN INITIATED	FIRST FLIGHT	INTO SERVICE	ORIGINAL ARMAMENT	FINAL ARMAMENT
Bell P-39	Mid-1930s	April 1938	Mid-1941	1 37 m/m 2 synch .50s 2 synch .30s	1 37 m/m 2 synch .50s 2 wing .50s
Grumman F4F	July 1936	Sept 1937	Dec 1940	2 synch .30s 2 wing .50s	6 wing .50s
Lockheed P-38	1937	Jan 1939	1941	1 23 m/m 4 .50s	1 20 m/m 4 .50s
Curtiss P-40	Early 1938	Late 1938	1941	2 synch .50s 2 wing .30s	6 wing .50s
Vought F4U	Feb 1938	May 1940	Oct 1942	1 synch .30 1 synch .50 2 wing .50s	6 wing .50s Later four 20 m/m cannon
Republic P-47	Mid-1940	May 1941	Nov 1942	8 wing .50s	8 wing .50s
N.A. P-51	April 1940	Oct 1940	April 1942 (with RAF)	2 synch .50s 2 wing .50s 4 wing .30s	6 wing .50s
Grumman F6F	June 1941	June 1942	Mid-1943	6 wing .50s	6 wing .50s

and in industry who felt that the biplane fighter was still the best answer. This attitude resulted in the Gloster Gladiator being accepted and ordered into production at a time when it was already hopelessly out of date. A handfull of gallant RAF airmen were soon to accomplish incredible feats in the Gladiator, over Malta and Greece — not because of their mount, but in spite of it.

The Gladiator's armament was a slight departure in that it was doubled, originally with two fuselage mounted Vickers and two underwing Lewis guns, all in the usual .303 caliber.

Two years before the Gladiator entered service the Armament Research Division of the Air Ministry had conducted extensive tests on all of the important aircraft guns of the world. The results of the tests spelled the end of the Vickers as an aircraft gun, as the U. S. Colt-Browning was obviously superior to anything else tested.

The Colt-Brownings used in the test were in the standard U. S. .30-06 caliber, and the Colt Company was queried as to the feasibility of converting them to fire the British .303 rimmed cartridge. In the early part of 1934 the Colt Company confirmed that the change in caliber could be easily made. The Air Ministry, therefore, began plans to adopt the Browning for most of its upcoming fighters and bombers.

In the mid-1930s armament installation designers were faced with several alternatives — each with its own advantages and disadvantages. To all except the most hidebound it was obvious that the biplane fighter had reached the end of the line. The monoplane was usually not as maneuverable, but in all respects it made the biplane look like what it was, an antique from the Great War. Along with the coming change there would be a need for much more powerful armament, but in what form? More guns? Faster firing guns? Cannon? All were coming and the armament engineer had to sort out the best for his own project — subject of course to the desires of the using air force.

The traditional cowl guns were burdened with a synchronizing device which often became out-of-adjustment due to wear, leaks in the hydraulic system, and inadequate maintenance. The inevitable result was a shattered or holed propeller. In addition to this, as the faster firing guns came into use it became more difficult to achieve reliable synchronization without slowing the rate of fire.

However, the cowl mounted guns, being close to the fuselage center line, had very little dispersal of their bullets out to the maximum effective range. The full weight of fire of both guns could be brought to bear on a target at widely varying ranges. In some air forces there was considerable reluctance to lose this advantage. The RAF was not one of these air forces.

In the spring of 1934, about the same time the changeover to Browning guns was decided upon, the Air Ministry issued specification F 5/34 which called for a fighter aircraft with a battery of 6 or 8 fixed guns. In the design stage at that time was a fighter which was not only a radical departure from the past, but also an aircraft which would soon play a leading role in the coming drama of WW-II — the Hawker Hurricane.

Although originally laid out as a four gun fighter, the licensing agreement between Colt and Birmingham Small Arms (BSA) in the summer of 1935, set the stage for revision of the Hawker's armament to eight .303 Browning, four in each wing, all firing clear of the propeller and eliminating the need for synchronization.

The ammunition bays of the 8 gun Hurricane I held 2660 rounds, sufficient for about 14 seconds of firing time. The short period of sustained fire indicated that a fighter pilot learn to fire — and get hits — in short bursts. It did not take many long bursts to expend the supply, leaving the hapless fighter pilot defenseless and tactically useless.

The Hurricane first flew in November, 1935 and entered service with #111 Squadron RAF near the end of 1937.

The Supermarine Spitfire, similar in layout and armament to the Hurricane but superior in performance, had entered development slightly later. It was, however, in production by the summer of 1938, and #19 Squadron at Duxford was the first to receive these historic machines in August of that year.

It was these two 8-gun fighters, powered by Rolls Royce Merlin engines, which were to fight, and win, one of the most dramatic of histories conflicts — the Battle of Britain.

As we have seen, the two principle British fighters emerging in the mid and late 1930s had made a clean break with tradition. There would be no more cowl-mounted guns on British fighters. However, the imposing battery of wing guns had its disadvantages also. Whereas with the old cowl guns, there was a minimum amount of bullet dispersion, with wing guns there was an excessive amount.

With four guns in each wing, there was considerable distance between them, and the guns were, in all cases, adjusted with their muzzles pointed in toward the aircraft center line. The fire of the guns therefore converged at a selected range, but at all closer, or further points, a target could be hit with only a portion of the total weight of fire. However, the guns could be harmonized to achieve a relatively good pattern over a long range.

The RAF, whose fighter armament had been submerged in the doldrums for more then 15 years after WW-I, was now making giant strides in the field. At about the same time development had begun on the revolutionary 8-gun Hurricane, work was proceeding on far more powerful armament that would rapidly relegate the rifle caliber guns to history in the short span of a few years. These guns were the automatic rapid fire cannon which had finally reached a stage of development that made them practical weapons. With the coming of the monoplane all-metal fighter, there was now an airframe in which they could be used successfully. These same type all-metal fighters in the enemy inventory also required the greater punch of the cannon for destructive results in the short times available that a target could be hit.

Strangely enough, while the British had made great strides in fighter armament over a short period, first with the multi-gun wing

This striking photo of an early P-39 with all guns firing was actually taken on the ground, but clever darkroom work produced this excellent "air" photo.   Textron's Bell Aerospace Co.

installations, and then their virtual replacement with cannon, none of the actual guns involved were British designed.

The 8-gun Hurricanes (some later had 12) and Spitfires of Battle of Britain fame were armed with Brownings differing only in caliber from the standard U. S. gun. The cannon, all in 20 m/m (about .78 inch) were Oerlikon and Hispano Suiza (often, like the engines of the same name, called "Hisso").

The latter was by far the most widely used 20 m/m gun in the British and U. S. services, while the Oerlikon was more common in the German and Japanese aircraft. Although of the same caliber, the ammunition for the two type guns was not interchangeable, cartridge case shape being different.

The Hispano was the product of a mixture of nationalities. Apparently invented by an Italian, and developed by Swiss engineers, it received its name from the famous European builder of automobiles, aircraft engines and armament.

Originally the Hisso cannon was designed for fitting between the banks of a V-type engine, firing through the hollow prop shaft. It was fed by a 60-round drum magazine. Its weight was slightly over 100 pounds and its rate of fire approximately 500-600 rounds per minute.

It is interesting to note that the 20 m/m projetcile had almost the same muzzle velocity and trajectory as the U. S. caliber .30 ammunition, but with a projectile weight 13 times greater.

The Hispano Suiza is a gas unlocked blowback type. Powder gases tapped off near the breech operate a piston which unlocks the breech block while there is still considerable pressure in the chamber. It is this remaining pressure which blows the breech block open, extracting and ejecting the empty cartridge case. The firing mechanism is cocked as the block opens and as it returns to the closed position, a cartridge is stripped from the magazine, and chambered ready for the next firing cycle.

Since we have not already done so, brief mention should be made of the difference between a machine gun and an automatic cannon. Both operate in a similar manner but the cannon normally fires an explosive projectile, while the machine gun does not — although there are exceptions on both sides.

In Britain the Hispano cannon was first used to arm the Westland Whirlwind, which became the first of the full cannon-armed fighters to enter service in quantity. Designed in 1935/36, the Whirlwind was a lean and handsome twin-engined machine with its four cannon grouped in the nose just forward of the cockpit. At the time of its first flight in 1938 and entry into service in 1940, the Whirlwind, whose guns provided a weight of fire per minute of 600 pounds, was by far the most effective in the world. The belt feed had not yet been developed and the ammunition supply was severely limited, being only the 60 rounds per gun contained in the drum magazines.

Although apparently a good enough fighter, the Whirlwind was, for various reasons, not produced in important quantities. Those that were, however, were used for some time, against ground and maritime targets in France and along the Channel coast, where the cannon were quite effective.

The origin of the Whirlwind's Hispano cannon is not known, but it may have been the parent company. A license to manufacture the gun had been obtained by BSA, and a factory had been built for its manufacture at Sparkbrook, but the first guns were not delivered to the RAF until the spring of 1940, some four months before the Battle of Britain.

After the BSA-built cannon entered service there was a great deal of difficulty with it. In July, 1940, Spitfire 1B's armed with a cannon in each wing began to arrive at #19 Squadron, and while the heavier punch of the 20 m/m was appreciated, the guns were far too unreliable for #19 to accept them willingly. As with many automatic weapons, the feed mechanism was the major fault, with an unsatifactory ejector adding to the troubles. Although #19 Squadron continued to utilize some of the cannon-armed Spits during the Battle of Britain, they remained extremely unreliable.

It would be well into the following year that the now reliable Hispano cannon became almost universal armament for the Spitfire Mk V, although it did retain four .303 Brownings.

About that same time, the Hurricane IIc began to enter squadron service. This mark had made a complete break with the rifle-caliber gun and its sole armament was four 20 m/m Oerlikon (later Hispano). Although the now outmoded Hurricane began to slowly fade from first line service, the major British fighters, the Spitfire, Typhoon and Tempest, continued to use the Hispano as their major armament until the end of WW-II. Alone of the three, the Spitfire often retained either .303 or .50 Brownings in addition to the cannon.

In Nazi Germany, in the early 1930s, Hitler was preparing another nightmare for Europe. A resurrection of the WW-I U-boat fleet, a powerful army and air force were again the main instruments to launch the coming aggression and great efforts were made to build up these forces.

Oddly enough, German military aircraft of the period bore a close resemblence to those emerging in England at the same time. The Me-109 was surprisingly similar to the Hurricane, and Luftwaffe bombers were of the same general layout and performance as their RAF counterparts.

The armament of these aircraft however, followed a different trend than that of the RAF, which had completely abandoned synchronized guns after the Gladiator. There were only two single-seat Luftwaffe fighters of any importance (except for the later jets) and these retained an armament layout which was a combination of wing and cowl guns.

German aircraft weapons of WW-II were designated differently than in WW-I. The letters MG followed by a series of numbers indicated a machine weapon of 20 m/m or less. Those above 20 m/m were identified by the letters MK. Sometimes the first two numbers after the letters gave the gun's caliber, but more often did not.

The MG-15 was one of the earliest used by the Luftwaffe. It was chambered for the standard German 7.92 m/m rifle cartridge, and was simply a modification of the infantry machine gun built by the Rheinmetall-Borsig firm. It was used both as a fixed gun and flexibly mounted in early WW-II bombers.

The MG-17 was a fixed gun which replaced the MG-15, and was similar to it, except it had been redesigned to fire from a closed bolt. This refers to the position the bolt is held in when the gun is not firing. The MG-15, and many other ground machine guns fire from an open bolt. This means that when the trigger is pulled, the bolt closes, chambering a cartridge, and firing it. The main advantage here is that when the gunner stops firing, cooling air can circulate through the barrel and chamber, and since no cartridge is chambered, there is no danger of "cookoff" (firing of a cartridge by heat). Since fixed aircraft guns generally receive plenty of cooling air blast, this feature is not needed.

The only other rifle-caliber gun in wide use was the MG-81, which was a Mauser product. This was a belt-fed gun used mostly in pairs, in gunners' position in bombers. Its rate of fire was quite high — around 1400 RPM.

The M2 Browning caliber .50 machine gun, as used in fixed fighter mounts. The barrel casing was peculiar to the P-47 Thunderbolt. It is being worked on here by two armourers of the 1st Brazilian Fighter Squadron which operated with U. S. forces in Italy.   Air Force Photo

The mighty Thunderbolt, the only U. S. single-engine 8-gun fighter. This one from the 9th Air Forces 358th Fighter Group has made an emergency landing after apparently being damaged by flak.
Air Force Photo

With the appearance of all-metal aircraft in the 1930s, it became obvious that the rifle-caliber machine gun could not accomplish the mission for many more years, and the armament sections of most air forces were already well underway with bigger guns at the time of the German attack in 1939. In Germany this included a 13 m/m Rheinmetall gun (roughly equivalent to the U. S. .50 Browning) and two different cannon of 20 m/m, all of which saw wide spread use during 1940-45.

The 13 m/m MG-131 was phased into service in 1938, and was used in bombers as a flexible weapon. Another important application of the MG-131 was as the cowl synchronized guns on both the Fw 190 and Me 109. Unlike most machine guns of that era, its ammunition was detonated electrically instead of by a mechanical firing pin.

The Swiss Oerlikon was the basis for the 20 m/m MG FF, shortened and modified by Rheinmetall. The FF was a designation of the Swiss Oerlikon company and retained by the Germans. The Oerlikon was a simple blowback action and in the short-barreled versions gave a muzzle velocity of less then 2,000 FPS, considerably below that of the Hispano and Mauser type.

Probably the best aircraft gun used by the Germans was the MG 151/20, designed and built by Waffenfabrik Mauser A.G. The unusual designation shows it to have been originally developed as a 15 m/m gun, but this was abandoned and the caliber rate increased to 20 m/m. The outstanding feature of this cannon was its high rate of fire, usually given as 780 RPM. Like the MG 131, it used electrically detonated ammunition, and provided a muzzle velocity of about 2,600 FPS.

The fighter that bore the brunt of the fighting during the early Hitler aggressions was the Me 109E, whose performance was superior to the RAF's Hurricane I, and roughly equal to the Spitfire. As originally designed in 1934 the 109 had only two cowl mounted rifle-caliber guns. Trends in England were clear however, and it was obvious that the 109 would be hopelessly outgunned by the 8 weapons of the new British fighters. The Luftwaffe was loath to part with its synchronized guns however, and although the airplane had a bewildering combination of weapons throughout its service life, the cowl guns remained a part of it. They were usually MG 17's, later replaced by the 13 m/m MG 131.

Besides the cowl mounted guns, most 109's had a single cannon mounted between the cylinder banks of the inverted Daimler Benz engine and firing through the hollow prop shaft. The MG 151/20 was the most common here. Weapons of various sizes were sometimes mounted in underwing gondolas, but the effect of these on performance was marked, and the 109 went through most of its operational life with three guns.

The early history of the Fw 190 is much the same, and although it also retained its cowl guns (13 m/m), it employed much more effective armament then the 109 in its later versions. These included a 20 m/m MG FF at about the mid-point of each wing, and an MG 151/20 Mauser in each wing root. These latter two were so close inboard that they required synchronization. The outboard Oerlikons were fed by the usual 60 round drum magazine, while the MG 151/20s were belt-fed.

The Luftwaffe never did field a successful heavy bomber, but relied upon the twin-engine medium. For the most part these were undergunned and generally a poor match for British and American fighters.

Armament and aircraft mechanics labor on a P-38 of the 474th Fighter Group somewhere in France. Air Force Photo

Some power operated turrets were used, but never reached the level of development that they did in Britain and the U. S. The most common German turret was the electrically driven DL 131, which mounted a single MG 131, and was power operated in azimuth only, the gunner supplying the muscle for elevation. This turret can be seen in photos of Do 217's and on some Ju 188's and He 177's. The latter aircraft, certainly one of the most technically interesting of the WW-II era, also mounted a 4-gun tail turret. The He 177 was, however, an endless source of trouble to the Germans and one which they probably wished they had never heard of.

The only other turret was the electro-hydraulic HD 151, a more satisfactory unit then the DL 131, it mounted a single 20 m/m cannon.

Remotely controlled turrets, or barbettes, were used on German aircraft, the best known being those on the aft fuselage of the Me 210 and 410 twin-engined fighters. These were built around the MG 131, and were meant to cover the area around the tail.

By the mid-war years, all of the major armament firms in Germany were either building, or in the design stage on, aircraft cannon larger then 20 m/m. 30 m/m was the most common, typified by the MK 108 by Rheinmetall. Four of these comprised the armament of the Me 262 jet fighter, and the Me 163 rocket fighter. It was the most widely used of the 30 m/m type and its most striking identification feature was its stubby 23-inch barrel.

Space does not permit going into detail on the great variety of cannon under development for the Luftwaffe, but the Mauser-built MG 213 deserves mention although it saw no service. This was a gas operated gun which used a five-shot revolving cylinder, much as in the familiar revolving pistol. It did not progress beyond the prototype stage, but was apparently the origin of the U. S. M39 revolving cannon used in the F-100 and other "century series fighters."

Fighter armament in the U. S. services during 1940-45 can easily be summed up in one phrase — caliber .50 M2 Browning. This was the only gun of any importance in this category. There was a transition phase in the late 1930s, on the eve of war, where there was a mixture of caliber .30 and .50, along with a few synchronized guns. By the mid-war years, most of these were gone and all important U. S. single engine fighters were armed with wing mounted .50s only. The only exception to this is the Bell P-39, and its importance is open to question.

The 20 m/m cannon did not reach a position of prominence. The American armament philosophy preferred the somewhat smaller caliber .50 projectile over the 20 m/m, because of the former's higher rate of fire. The North American Mustang will be discussed as generally typical of U. S. fighters of WW-II.

The author must confess to a considerable fondness for the metal Mustang of a quarter of a century ago. He was closely associated with the machine, and the men who flew and maintained her with the old 8th Air Force. He was impressed then, and remains so today.

The P-51's armament was not so impressive however, and went through several changes before reaching a satisfactory stage. The early Allison powered P-51's mounted the usual combination of those days, but the last with this engine switched to four .50 wing guns only, which remained standard through the Merlin-powered B and C models. The guns did not sit upright on their mounts, but were inclined almost on their sides. The ammunition cans were outboard of the guns and the ammo belts crossed over the top of the gun and fed into the feed mechanism from a very sharp curve.

A P-51B of the China-based 14th Air Force. The muzzles of the generally unsatisfactory gun installation can be seen just above the tube type rocket launchers. Air Force Photo

There was a great deal of trouble in combat in that the belt links broke from violent maneuvers, and the guns often jammed from poor feeding and ejection provisions. It was not uncommon for 8th AF P-51's to return from a mission with half or more of their guns out of action. Another common problem was freezing of the oil on the gun bolt, and also freezing of the firing solenoid. In the 357th Group, the latter problem was solved by covering the solenoid with a heavy wrapping of tape and a coat of shellac.

With the P-51D, the designers finally corrected the poor gunnery system. Now there were six guns, mounted in an upright position, and there was little further trouble. Ammunition supply on the D model (and the similar K) was 400 rounds for each inboard gun, and 270 RPG for the center and outboard.

An N-1 gun camera was provided in the left wing root, and until the advent of the K-14 computing sight, the standard gunsight was the optical N-3B (P-51B and C) and the N-9 (P-51D and K).

FIGHTER GUN SIGHTS

"I was flying Dollar Red Three when we saw a gaggle of approximately 70 enemy aircraft about 6,000 feet below, going 180 degrees to us. I did a wingover and dove into the rear of the gaggle. I picked out an Fw 190 and at 300 yards began firing from dead astern. I got numerous strikes and he exploded at the cockpit. The pilot did not get out.

"I selected another Fw 190, who started evasive action, giving me a 20-degree angle off shot at him. I closed to 200 yards, firing numerous bursts and getting strikes all over his fuselage. He turned to the left and the pilot bailed out. My wingman, Lt. Hyman, observed this as he was on the inside of the turn.

"Singling out another 190, I commenced firing from 500 yards, closing to 100 yards, getting strikes on the wing roots and cockpit. When I overshot to the right, the pilot rolled over and bailed out. My wingman did not observe this because he was off to my right.

"There was still plenty of enemy aircraft around, so I got on my fourth 190. While I was trying to get a shot however, a 190 slid onto my tail and began firing. My wingman, Lt. Hyman, shot him off. I observed this because the plane snapped over and went down, and I saw either the canopy or a wing fall off the plane. Then I managed to get a shot at the 190 in front of me. I saw hits on the wing and cockpit. He started smoking and went into an uncontrollable

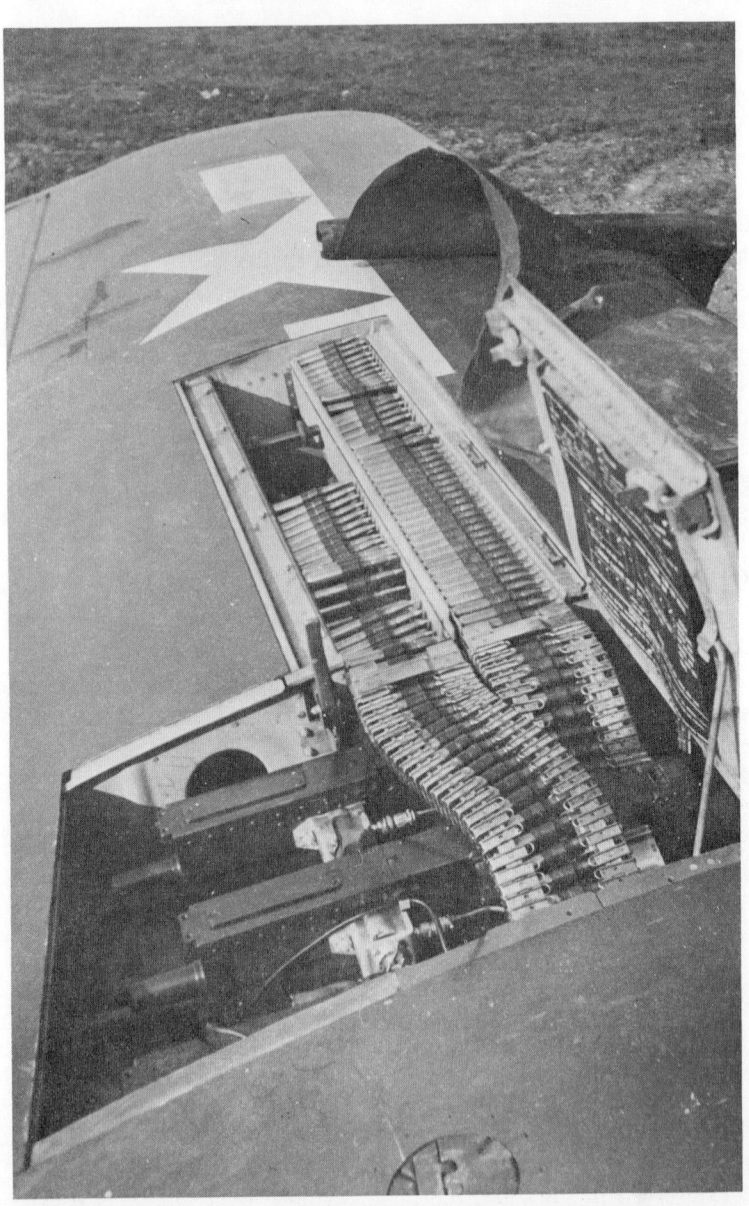

The final production P-51 Mustang armament installation, three caliber .50's in each wing, is seen here in a P-51D of the 8th Air Force in the summer of 1944. Author's Photo

The British designed K-14 computing gun sight, installed in a P-51D of the 357th Fighter Group of the 8th Air Force.   Author's Photo

Clark Field, Philippines, summer 1945. A P-51D of the 41st Fighter Squadron has its guns boresighted.   Air Force Photo

spin and crashed. The pilot did not get out.

"I pulled up and started for home because I was hit in the left wing. My aileron and compass had been damaged."

The above words are those of 2nd Lt. Otto "Dittie" Jenkins, and graphically reveal a picture of a fighter pilot doing what he is expected to do — shoot down enemy aircraft.

The above described action took place near Fulda, Germany on the afternoon of the 24th of December, 1944. "Dittie" Jenkins was a member of the famed "Yoxford Boys," the 357th Fighter Group of the 8th Air Force. He was to die in a crash at home base three months later.

Many thousands of fighter pilots over the years have not been as successful as Jenkins — even those who had the opportunities. Besides the usual piloting skills, and the vital aggressiveness, the fighter pilot had to have a thorough knowledge of gunnery principles because he always had a lot going against him.

We have discussed fighter armament over the years, and even had a few words to say about the gun sights of 1914-18. To better understand fighter armament of the WW-II era we must take a look at the gun sights and gunnery problems of those days also.

One of the most famous and long-lived of naval fighters was the Chance Vought Corsair. This one is the F4U-5 night fighter version, armed with four 20 m/m AN-M2 cannon with flash hiders.   Chance Vought Photo

The standard fighter gun sights during most of WW-II were the simple optical reflector sight where a ring of light and a center bead are projected onto a reflector plate — a transparent mirror through which the pilot looks to line up the target with the ring of light. The most common types in use with U. S. services were the N3-A, L3-B, the N-9 and the Mk 8, all of which were very similar.

Which ever sight was used it was necessary that sight, gun, and aircraft be lined up — or harmonized. Only when these were properly co-ordinated, did the fighter pilot have an efficient fighting weapon.

Although we usually think of the fire of wing guns of the WW-II era fighter as converging to meet at a specified point in space along the flight path, this was not always the case. There were two types of harmonization, the one referred to above was called "point harmonization," and it resulted in the heaviest possible concentration of fire at certain ranges. However, it also resulted in excessive dispersion at most ranges; and the more common method was "pattern harmonization," which gave the best pattern of a uniform lethal density over the entire effective range of the guns. 2,000 feet was maximum effective range for harmonization, but in actual practice, 1200 to 1500 feet was the maximum, and most firing was done at much less.

With the guns, airplane and sight properly aligned, it was now

Grumman's rugged F6F Hellcat was the mainstay of U. S. carrier fighter squadrons. This one, belonging to Carrier Aircraft Service Unit 47, has belly-landed on Okinawa in Sept. 1944. Aviation Ordnancemen are clearing the wing guns of live ammunition. Author's Photo

entirely up to the fighter jockey to get results. Quite often it was still difficult!

When firing at a target dead ahead, the fighter pilot's biggest problem was figuring the range and the best time to open fire. With practice this was relatively easy, but in air combat many targets were not dead ahead and this introduced a bigger problem and one which is familiar to all skilled wild game hunters — that of lead, or deflection allowance. If the target is moving across in front of the gunner, he must shoot not at the target, but where it will be when the projectiles reach that point in space. In order to figure the proper amount of lead, it was necessary for the gunner (fighter pilot) to estimate the angle between himself and the target, the speed and size of the target, and its range.

All of which is a fair indication of why a great many fighter pilots were not *successful* fighter pilots!

Help was on the way for the American fighter pilot however, and arrived in the fall of 1944 in the form of a gyro computing gunsight which did much of the problem solving within its own black box. This was the K-14 sight which was much more then a new gadget. Delighted fighter pilots soon found that it was possible to get five times as many hits with the K-14 as with the older fixed sights, and the percentage of fighter victories in the ETO tripled after its introduction.

These almost fantastic improvements in gunnery make the K-14 worth a longer look. Like many other aeronautical improvements of that era, the K-14 was a British development where it was first used in bombers as the Mk IIc turret sight.

The drawings of this sight were turned over to the 8th Air Force, by the RAF, in June of 1944, and were sent to the states for manufacture. When the first production K-14 sights arrived at 8th Air Force fighter stations later in the summer it was found that they had been built for the P-51B, an aircraft rapidly being replaced by the D model, on which the K-14 would not fit. (The windshield had a greater slope, and therefore, less clearance beneath it for the sight).

The commander of the author's old group (the 357th Fighter), Colonel Donald Graham, decided not to waste time returning the sights to the U. S. for modification, and turned them over to the Group's armament section. In a few days, a trial P-51D had been modified, a new mount built, and the K-14 went to war with the 357th. An immediate success, Colonel Graham ordered enough

The Bell Airacobra was unique in many ways, one of which was the fact that it mounted guns of three different calibers. This is the British P-400 version in service with the U. S. 67th Fighter Sqdn. on Henderson Field, Guadalcanal.   Marine Corps Photo

mounts built to equip all of the Group's P-51's.

Although North American and 8th Air Force Engineering Section also designed new mounts for the K-14, none were as satisfactory as the locally built ones, and many 8th Air Force groups adopted the 357th unit.

In order to use the K-14, the pilot was required to feed in certain information for the computer to work on. The correct size

Probably the best of the Luftwaffe single-seat fighters was the Fw 190. This one carries only the cowl guns and the inboard cannon, the outboard weapons being deleted.   Author's Photo

(wingspan) of the target had to be set into the sight and this was done by a selector lever and scale on the front of the sight, facing the pilot. Early K-14s had a simple foot scale, which required the pilot to know the wingspan of all likely targets. This was later replaced with one marked by enemy aircraft type. (If the scale was set half way between "Me 109" and "Fw 190" it was suitable for both).

With the sight now informed of the target type (and size) the pilot had only to feed the range into the sight and it computed the correct lead angle. The range was fed into the unit by the pilot rotating the engine throttle grip (which had been replaced with a cylindrical shaped twist grip) which varied the diameter of a circle of light (actually six diamonds forming a circle) on the reflector. The pilot no longer had to aim ahead of the target, but only to keep it within the light circle, keeping its wing tips on the diamond points. After tracking for one second, he could begin firing — far more sure of hits then he had been with the old sights.

Captain John B. England, fighter pilot par excellence, of the 357th Group, was highly impressed with the K-14 sight as is easily seen in his encounter report for the 13th of September, 1944. This action took place south of Nordhausen, Germany:

"I was leading Dollar Squadron at 8,000 feet when I spotted one Me 109 ahead and below us making a gentle dive toward a large city. I immediately dove after him and started closing to about 800 yards at 3,000 feet. The enemy pilot then saw me and started a break into me and was headed for a large airdrome. I was traveling at approximately 400 miles per hour and made a very tight turn into him and closed to about 500 yards. I placed the enemy aircraft properly within my K-14 sight and squeezed the trigger. I got strikes all over the engine and cockpit. The enemy aircraft, burning and smoking excessively went out of control and crashed into a river 1,000 feet below.

"Without the K-14 sight and my 'G' suit I don't believe I would have gotten this Jerry as he was headed for a heavily defended airdrome. My wing man said later that I was pulling six 'G's' when I got this Jerry.

"About twenty minutes after my first encounter I was leading my squadron up to escort the last box of bombers that were withdrawing. We were jumped by eight-plus Me 109's at 15,000 feet. I tacked on to three that were spiraling toward the deck. I lined up on the leader's wing man and closed to about 300 yards and started

One of the last of the German piston-engined fighters was the strange twin-engined Dornier 335, but it retained the three-gun layout of the earlier Luftwaffe fighters. The blast trough for the cowl gun can be seen as well as the cannon port in the spinner. Author's Photo

firing. He tried both left and right evasive turns, but as I had him in my K-14 sight his efforts were in vain. Finally he made a tight pull-out on the deck and cut his throttle. I cut my throttle and finished him off. I closed to 100 yards, his canopy came off, smoke and pieces flew by. He rolled over and exploded in some woods below. Immediately after this Jerry exploded, I made a 180-degree turn and caught another Jerry who was very aggressive. We spent about five minutes in a tight Lufberry at tree top altitude. I finally got in position for my first burst. I observed strikes around his tail section and one of his wheels dropped. I overshot him and pulled up sharp. My wing man, Lt. Fuller, came in and got some good strikes on him and the enemy aircraft started smoking. My wing man overshot and I came back and was getting strikes on him when he crashed into the side of a hill and exploded. At one time in this last encounter I got strikes from a 90-degree deflection shot using the K-14 sight."

The K-14 gunsight for fighters remained in use for many years, and survived the changeover from piston engine to jet propelled aircraft. The U. S. Navy used the sight in large numbers and they were seen in French Navy Corsairs (F4U) at the time that aircraft were phased out of service. The author has seen them quite recently

Belonging to 41 Squadron, RAF, this Spitfire XII was photographed in December, 1943. The starboard cannon and two machine gun ports can be seen in the wing leading edge. Author's Photo

in armed Lockheed T-33s, and some of the older fighter types still in service.

The very similar K-15 sight was a bomber turret unit. The earlier turret computing sights such as the K-3 type were only accurate as long as the bomber was flying straight and level. The K-15 worked equally well during evasive action or straight and level flight, and was used in increasing numbers from the fall of 1944 until the end of the war in Europe.

IV
BOMBERS OF WORLD WAR TWO

Throughout the history of bombardment aviation from the single engine two seaters of WW-I, through the multi-engine, multi-seat bombers of the 1920s and early 1930s, there had been little change in defensive armament.

In the Great War, the French had called the gunners cockpit ring a *tourelle*. The British called it a Scarff Ring. The Americans used both terms and obviously the Germans had another name. Regardless of the name they all served the same purpose — to mount a machine gun (sometimes two) that could be moved about freely by the gunner. Probably the best of the lot was the British Scarff ring, invented by a warrant officer of the RNAS, and used by all the Allied Services. It was well into the 1930s before the Scarff ring was relegated to the museums.

Even then, when the new monoplane two and four-engine bombers were beginning to enter service, the traditional gunner with his single free firing rifle-caliber gun remained as part of the scene. As airspeeds crept upward it had become more difficult for the unfortunate gunner to swing his weapons against the slipstream. This was one of the major lessons in aircraft design from WW-I, but little attention was paid to it for many years. In the United States, Air Service tests in the 1920s showed that it took 106 pounds of force to swing two Lewis guns against a 160 mph slipstream. Various methods utilizing springs, worm gears and windvane compensators were tried over the years in order to assist the gunner. Most of the effort was wasted as none were successful.

The ultimate answer in the form of a power operated turret in which man, guns, and sighting equipment all operated as a unit, was well known, but usually rejected — in the U.S. at least. One type of patented turret was turned down by the Chief of Air Service armament Section for being too heavy and complicated and "because it is power operated, which seems unnecessary in a device to carry a machine gun for defensive purposes."

Since the aircraft of the 1920s and early 1930s varied little from those of 1918, there was little incentive to provide new armament. By the mid 1930s however, change was taking place.

In many new bombers the gunner was no longer standing in a hole in the fuselage, swinging his gun on a Scarff ring. The designers still were hesitant about giving him a power turret because of weight, complexity, and effect on aircraft performance, but they were now willing to put the gunner inside with the rest of the crew. His gun was now mounted at an opening in the fuselage, increasing his sense of security, but decreasing his field of fire considerably. The weapon remained a single rifle-caliber gun in most cases.

In Europe, the shape of the WW-II type turret began to emerge early in the 1930s. In France, England and Italy, the domed plastic cover began to appear, but most of these required long vertical slots for the gun barrels, and offered little protection for the gunner.

In the U. S. the domed plastic cover was first used on the nose turret of the Martin B-10 which entered service with the 2nd Bomb Group at Langley Field in the winter of 1935-36. The turret, however, was still a manually operated unit.

The Italians seem to have been the first to come forth with the right idea of turret layout where the twin guns were widely spaced in the turret, leaving room between the gun breeches for the gunner and sighting equipment. By 1937 th American military attache in Rome reported power turrets were in use in most Italian bombers.

In the United Kingdom also, there had been much activity in turret design, starting about 1930, so that by the time the Bristol Blenheim bomber appeared in 1936, its main defensive armament was a hydraulically operated upper turret with a .303 gun.

In the U. S., which was to see the highest point of turret development in a few short years, Bomber armament had lagged far behind. American bombers in September, 1939, the same month that Europe went to war, mounted the following defensive armament:

Martin B-10 (contracted for March '31; first production July '34)
1 nose .30 caliber manual turret
1 upper .30 caliber hand held
1 lower .30 caliber hand held

Boeing B-17 (contracted for October '35; first production November '38)
1 nose .30 caliber hand held
1 upper .30 caliber hand held
1 lower .30 caliber hand held
2 waist .30 caliber hand held

Douglas B-18 (contracted for January '36; first production June '37)
1 nose .30 caliber manual turret
1 upper .30 caliber manual turret
1 lower .30 caliber hand held

Douglas B-23 (contracted for June '37; first production November '37)
1 nose .30 caliber hand held
1 upper .30 caliber hand held
1 lower .30 caliber hand held
1 tail .50 caliber hand held

There was not a power turret among them, and but one caliber .50 gun. Of these four bombers, three were obsolete and only the B-17 was to see combat in quantity.

The lack of progress in U. S. bomber armament is strange when it becomes clear that the bomber was considered the most important weapon in the Army Air Corps, and in fact, the faith placed in the bombers ability to defend itself would seriously hamper fighter design in the U. S. until well into WW-II. Although the theory of long range, high altitude precision bombing was well implanted, the Army had never had the bombers to carry it out. That realization was becoming clear in the 1930s.

War in Europe was already looming on the horizon when the Material Division of the Air Corps expressed the need for power-operated turrets on bombers. This was 1939 and the beginning of a five year experimental program. However, the Axis powers were about to shoot down the experimental program for the fiscal years 1940-44.

In that same year (1939) the Boeing B-17 was available in only very limited numbers. Yet it was to become one of the most important aircraft in the U. S. arsenal, and the development of its armament is highly interesting.

The B-17 was designed in response to AAC circular proposal 35-26. The year was 1935 and at that time the official type specification for multi-engined bombers called for installation of a minimum of three gun positions, all caliber .30 — a nose gun, an upper midship gun and a lower or floor gun. The addition of any further guns was opitional with the designer. Boeing elected to supply two further gun positions, one on each side of the fuselage called waist guns, and mounted in teardrop shaped blisters.

The Armament Branch at Wright Field was unhappy with the layout from the beginning, as expressed in a memo dated 1 October, 1935:

"Although the combined area covered by the three guns (2 waist and 1 upper) is undoubtedly greater than that which could be allocated to one retractable turret, it would require three gunners constantly stationed at these positions during an engagement. This number, in addition to nose and floor gunners, would be in excess of those who could be allotted for defense out of a crew of five." Before it was over the B-17 would require a crew double that size.

Regardless of the displeasure of the Armament Branch, the B-17 was built with five gun positions. 18 months later, after firing tests at Langley Field showed a very limited field of fire, the Armament Branch again expressed its opinion that any future large airplanes be required to have "one well-designed power-driven turret located in the upper rear position." Over the next several years the Armament Branch continued to criticize the B-17, but with frustrattingly little success. The airplane progressed steadily through the D series with substantially the same armament. Another serious deficiency was the lack of a tail gun. Only one American bomber of the late 1930s had a tail gun. This was the Douglas B-23 and Wright Field found the installation barely adequate. Boeing had resisted suggestions for a tail gun on the B-17 with the reply that it would require a complete redesign of the aft fuselage.

It would be 1941, with the appearance of the E series that the Flying Fortress would begin to look like its name, and its crew had doubled to include four full-time gunners and three part-time.

In the summer of 1940, the RAF was engaged in its gigantic struggle with the Luftwaffe for control of the skies over the Island Kingdom. RAF bombers played a decidedly secondary role during this period. Yet the defensive armament of British bombers was far advanced over that of the United States and this was to serve as a much needed prod to American military planners and designers.

RAF bombers already in service, such as the Wellington and the Whitley were equipped with both nose and tail power turrets, each with two .303 Brownings.

There appeared also in that spring of 1940, a bomber that was a milestone in RAF history. This was the Short Stirling, which although handicapped by many deficiencies, was the first of the RAF's true "heavies." It was the result of an Air Ministry specification in 1936 which called for a bomber with range and bomb capacity far beyond anything in existence at that time.

From the defense armament standpoint, the Stirling was another first — there were no hand-held machine guns (although some were added later), its defensive capabilities were embodied in three hydraulic power-operated turrets, the nose with two .303s, the tail with four, and a twin-gun Boulton Paul turret in the dorsal position.

The Stirling's shortcomings are beyond the scope of this book, but it was in 1940 the most heavily armed bomber in the world, and a tough opponent for Luftwaffe fighters of the period.

Better bombers were on the way for the RAF, but the gun layout pioneered by the Stirling remained standard for the remainder of WW-II. The best of the new bombers was the Avro Lancaster with four-gun nose and tail turrets and a twin-gun dorsal. Not until the advent of the Avro Lincoln near the end of WW-II, which mounted 20 m/m cannon in its turrets, did British bombers abandon the .303 Browning as standard.

Although far superior to Axis bombers in defensive firepower, the Halifax and Lancaster, the RAF's major heavy bombers, were badly undergunned and ill equipped to shoot it out with cannon-armed fighters. The RAF, however, had found out early in the war, that bombers operating in daylight would usually take unacceptable casualties from German fighters, and the vast percentage of RAF bombing operations were at night where the .303 caliber Brownings were not quite so much of a disadvantage.

As mentioned previously, the advanced state of British turret design was of great interest in the U. S. and there was considerable discussion in 1940 and 1941 as to whether it would be better to build British turrets under a license arrangement or to proceed with original designs. The latter course was the one finally adopted, and resulted in superior turrets.

British turrets were built in largest numbers by two companies.

Fraser-Nash turrets, built by Parnell Aircraft Ltd, consisted of four basic types, all hydraulically driven. These included both 4 and 2-gun nose and tail turrets and a retractable belly turret called a "dustbin."

The Boulton Paul turrets were similar, but used a self contained electro-hydraulic power unit. The Fraser-Nash drew its hydraulic fluid from the aircraft system and was much more easily put out of action by damage to the very long fluid lines required to reach the turrets.

It was this advanced state of British bomber armament and the European war in general which finally set in motion the events which would produce the world's most heavily armed bombers.

However, the entire subject of bomber armament in 1939-40 was in such a flux, it would take a large volume to cover the complexities of fire control and turret design, and the many blind alleys of research, as well as the successful ones. The changeover from caliber .30 to caliber .50 also raised many problems other then the size of the guns. Only the surface of this interesting period can be skimmed.

In 1939 and 1940 there were four U. S. companies actively engaged in design and construction of aircraft turrets. They were: Sperry, whose equipment was in general earmarked for the B-17; General Electric, whose production was allocated to the Martin B-26 and the Douglas A-20; The Bendix Company, earmarked for the North American B-25; and the Martin Company itself which had designed its own turret for the B-26, using some GE components. The Westinghouse Company was also interested but was plagued by troubles which it never did solve.

All of these companies were treading new ground and there was a great deal of lost effort, which usually however, provided very valuable experience for the future.

One of the most vexing problems of turret design was the gulf between the shooting war and the designer's drawing board. Most of the latter had no combat experience of course, and as a consequence, turrets throughout WW-II lacked many things the gunners considered essential. Many were excessively cramped, had inadequate heating and intercom, and such a simple thing as canopy frame design often made scanning very difficult. These and many other technical problems were slowly solved over the years, although some remained to the end.

The Sperry Company, although not as large as GE and Bendix,

was one of the leaders in gun turret manufacture. Sperry was in fact, not able to handle the high volume production needed, and subcontractors such as Briggs Manufacturing Company, Steel Products Corp. and Emerson Electric built thousands of Sperry turrets.

By late 1940, the Sperry Company was ready to go into production on its powered upper turret and a remotely-controlled belly turret for the B-17. However, the remote belly turret was severely criticized by gunners after it was in production. The sighting head beneath the fuselage was often obscured with oil and exhaust stains, and the restricted vision cone of the remote sight made it difficult to pick up a target.

The hostile reception to the remote turret spurred Sperry to develop the soon to be famous ball turret, which was largely built by Sperry subcontractors, Briggs Manufacturing, and Emerson Electric. One of the biggest concerns of the AAF was in regard to the unusual "embryonic" position of the gunner in the ball turret. However, tests by Briggs showed only a small loss in efficiency over a period of several hours occupancy, and the ball turret went into production before it was even fully tested. (It is possible that ex-8th Air Force gunners might disagree with the findings of the Briggs tests!)

Firing tests of the Sperry ball in the summer of 1941 showed it to be an excellent unit, but it presented production difficulties which threatened its future. By January 1942 both Emerson and Briggs had overcome these and were in production on the unique ball turret which was to remain a feature of the B-17 throughout the rest of its combat life.

As with all American turrets of the era, the Sperry ball mounted two M2 caliber .50 Brownings. On the ground there was little clearance and the gun barrels could not be pointed down without striking the ground. The turret operated from a self contained hydraulic power source, and elevation and azimuth control was through a pair of handgrips, on top of which were mounted the firing buttons. Tracking of a target was accomplished with the hand controls while range information was fed into the computing gunsight by operation of a foot pedal, which adjusted the sight reticles to frame the target.

Although there were many minor modifications to the Sperry ball, there was only major change and this did not affect the B-17. This change was the addition of a hydraulic retracting mechanism, and it was used on the B-24 to reduce aerodynamic drag when the turret was not in use.

The ball turret effectively eliminated the traditional blind spot on bombers, but it was no place for a gunner with claustrophobia! Although the flight manual warned that it was never to be occupied on takeoff or landing, there was always the possibility of turret jamming and a trapped gunner.

The manual for the B-17 also recommended that the ball turret be dropped if a belly landing was necessary and time permitted (it took about 20 minutes to release it). It also suggests that, if feasible, the expensive computing gun sight be removed before dropping.

The B-17 was not only one of the most important of all U. S. WW-II aircraft, but also one of the most colorful. Throughout the first few years of its service it was badly undergunned, but by the time it began its association with the mighty 8th Air Force and began its epic battle in the hostile skies of Germany, it was no longer undergunned.

Because of its place in history we will examine the armament of the B-17G in some detail. Other then the ball turret, already discussed, these were two more power turrets, the upper, and the chin.

The upper turret was also a Sperry product, although many were built by Steel Products Company. It also operated from a self-contained hydraulic power system and was controlled in elevation and azimuth by a set of handlevers. Unlike the ball turret, range information for the computing gun sight was set-in by twisting the right-hand grip.

One of the most interesting of the design problems involved with the Sperry upper turret was the fire cutout or gun interrupter device. The purpose of this unit was to stop the guns firing whenever the muzzles were in line with any part of the aircraft.

This was accomplished by a profile cam which rotated with the turret and provided positive firing circuit interruption. As originally designed, however, both guns cut out at the same time, which deprived the gunner of all of his firepower at what could be critical times. After heated comments from the combat zones, the system was refined so that the leading gun cut out first as it swept toward the tail (for example) and then resumed firing the instant it was clear, while the following gun cut out and in a fraction of a second later. The cutout device provided protection for all parts of the aircraft which would be in the line of fire, including wing and horizontal stabilizer, forward fuselage and propeller discs.

An indication of how intricate the fire cut-out system was can be seen in another problem encountered soon after the Sperry upper turret was in service. It was found that when the turret was slewed (rotated) into a restricted area at high speed, the period elapsing between the time when the interrupter cam opened the circuit and the time when the last fired projectile actually left the gun, was enough to cancel out the interrupter system. In other words, turret slewing speed was sometimes fast enough for the gun barrels to have already entered the restricted zone before the gun stopped firing. The result was gunfire damage to some part of one's own aircraft. This was overcome with a device which advanced the interrupter cam as the turret increased rotational speed, somewhat like the spark advance on an automobile engine.

The chin turret was a feature added to B-17 production as a result of combat experience in Europe. Luftwaffe fighters had adopted a headon attack on bomber formations as they had found the nose to be weakly defended. Until the advent of the chin turret, the bombardier had only a pair (sometimes three) of hand held .50s to defend the nose.

The chin turret was an electrically operated unit built by Bendix. The bombadier was the chin turret gunner, and the weapons were again M2 caliber .50s, but there was no computing gun sight, a standard N-6 optical type being used.

The earliest chin turrets were actually modified Bendix remote lower units from B-25 production. This installation had been hope-

Boeing B-17G's enroute to Emden, Germany, 1944.   USAF Photo

less and it was hoped to salvage the turrets by modifying them for chin turret use on the B-17F.

A few trial installations and combat missions showed the old remote sight setup to be as bad as it had been on the B-25, and they were used on only a few B-17Fs. The production chin turrets for the B-17G employed direct sighting and were much more satisfactory.

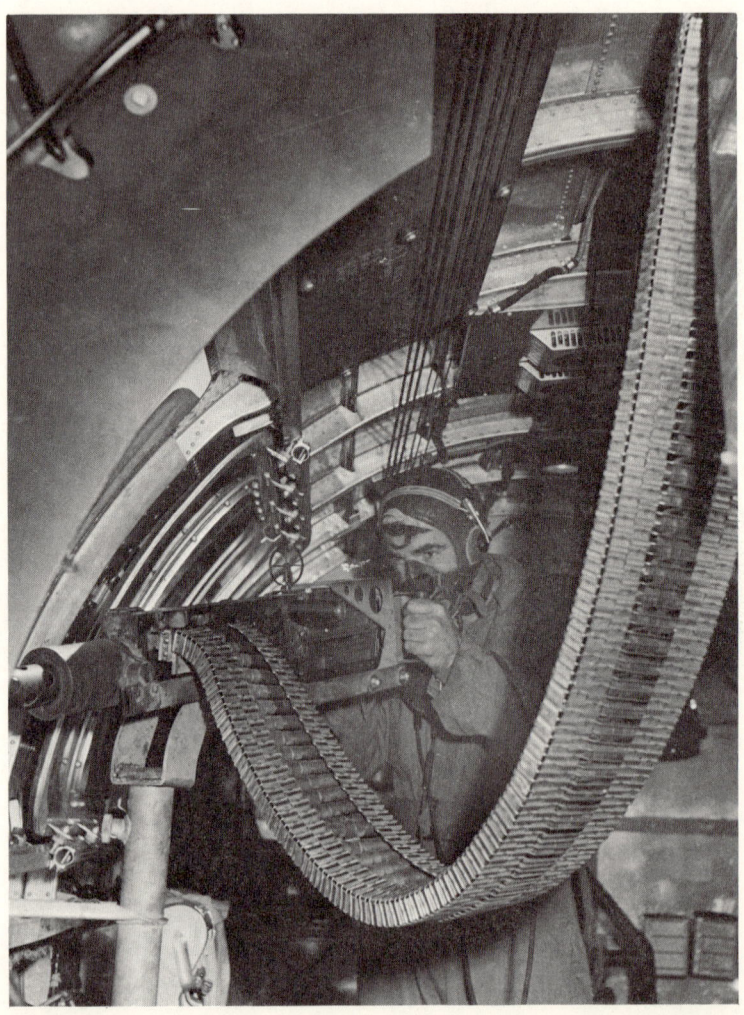

SSgt Bill Wise, right waist gunner, mans his flexible .50 machine gun in this interior shot of an 8th Air Force B-17G.   Air Force Photo

The remainder of the B-17's defensive armament was made up of five hand-held guns, two in a manual tail turret, one in each waist position — a carryover from the original design, and one with extremely limited field of fire in the radio compartment.

The B-17's stablemate in the heavy bomber role was the Consolidated B-24 Liberator. In 1939-40 when the Material Division of the Air Corps assigned the various turret contractors to develop armament for specific bombers, the B-24 had not been included. Possibly this is the reason that the B-24 eventually had such a hodge podge of different turrets.

Like the B-17, the '24 originally had no power turrets and was equally undergunned. When the fact became known that both British and German fighters were hacking undergunned bombers out of the sky in a most shocking fashion, design changes were begun to improve the B-24's ability to slash back.

These changes were too varied and too often to go into much detail, but the Lib eventually saw service with gun turrets from four different manufacturers! The nose turret, when it was eventually installed, was sometimes an Emerson unit, the upper turret a Martin, the ball turret a Sperry, and that in the tail, Consolidated's own design.

The Consolidated tail turret was one of the more unsatisfactory turrets of the period. It had been designed to a definite weight limitation and ended up with the fundamental fault of being too small for even a medium-sized man in flight gear.

Even though many modifications and improvements were incorporated, a report from the Air Corps Experimental Engineering Section noted that the turret was "still an inefficient combat weapon due to the instability of the gun mounts, sight vibration, and the lack of room."

Even though this may have been true, the turret remained in use till the end, and was even installed in the nose of some B-24s during 1943, until Bendix chin and Emerson nose turrets became available. Even with its faults, however, the Consolidated tail turret was available when needed and its firepower no doubt brought many a Liberator home that would not otherwise have made it.

Although the Forts and Libs served in many roles and many areas throughout WW-II, it was in Europe that they found their places in history. For it was here that the U. S. concept of a heavily-armed bomber defending itself against enemy fighters, was put to the

A rare photo of a B-24 modified with the GE gunnery system as used in the B-29, and used to train B-29 gunners. Ray Pritchard Photo

Liberators of 31 Squadron, Royal Australian Air Force. The nose turret here is an Emerson unit. RAAF official via Barry Pattison

test — and found wanting.

It is true that the heavies of the 8th Bomber Command were usually able to punch their way through to the target, and while doing so to inflict heavy losses on equally determined German fighters. But they could not do it without unacceptable losses to themselves, and so the concept changed. That change in concept eventually brought hordes of AAF fighters to England. These were the 8-gun Thunderbolt, the graceful Lightning, and finally the incomparable Mustang. With the latter the heavies now had an escort anywhere their mission took them. It was a combination the hard fighting Luftwaffe could not match, and it was overwhelmed and destroyed — on the ground and in the air.

Among the five major bombers in, or approaching production and service use in 1940 was the medium B-25 Mitchell, soon to roll from the lines at North American's Inglewood plant. As usual the original design was grossly undergunned, but eventually the B-25 packed the firepower unthought of in 1940.

This ingenious "in the field" installation of six caliber .50 Brownings on a B-25, was the work of the China-based 341st Bomb Group.
Air Force Photo

In the assignment of turret development by the Armament Lab at Wright Field, Bendix had drawn the B-25, and was hard at work on an upper and a remote retractable lower — both to mount the now standard twin .50s.

Bendix seems to have been plagued with unsolvable problems during much of its early turret work, and the B-25 was to suffer because of it. Bendix turrets were electrically-driven and for a long time B-25 gunners had to put up with a turret which had a dead spot in azimuth travel as the unit passed its neutral position. Such a dead spot made smooth tracking of a target impossible and increased the gunners' already numerous problems. The upper turret eventually became at least an acceptable weapon, but the lower remote never did make the grade.

An excessively long time (55 seconds) was required to extend it from a retracted position, and once in firing, the gunner, who knelt over a periscope sight, found it very difficult to pick up targets, and control was also bad on the lower. One report of the day summed it up thusly: "No matter who voiced the opinion, the Bendix lower turret was admittedly a collection of malfunctions."

Nevertheless, many Bendix lower remotes were built and installed in early B-25's. When the decision was made to halt their use on the B-25 in mid-1942, it was hoped those on hand could be modified for chins turrets on the B-17F. Here they were unsuccessful also, although the later chin turrets by Bendix for the B-17G and the B-24 gave good service.

Other then the development of the turbine (jet) aircraft engine, probably the most outstanding technical achievement on the WW-II aeronautical scene was the B-29 Superfortress. With the B-29, the state of WW-II aircraft armament also reached its most sophisticated level.

In the B-29, the USAAF finally had a bomber to fit the strategic warfare ideas the airmen had been cultivating for many years. The Superfortress was largely instrumental in the final defeat of the Japanese without any invasion by ground troops of the Japanese Home Islands.

Since the B-29 was the strapping descendent of the B-17, and the last of the multi-turret bombers to see combat, a closer look at the aircraft's armament is worth while. The development history of the '29 is well covered in several excellent books and it will not be gone into here except to say that the airplane was the end result of

The eternal symbol of 8th Bomber Command, the Boeing B-17. Upper, chin, and ball turrets can be seen on this 381st Bomb Group G model, photographed in July, 1944. Air Force Photo

a series of design studies by the Boeing Airplane Company to satisfy an Air Corps requirement for a very large, long-range heavy bomber with a pressurized crew compartment. Powered by four of the new, relatively untried, and often incredibly unreliable Wright R-3350 engines, the B-29 first flew in September of 1942. The Air Corps, which had ordered it into quantity production long before the first flight, envisioned it as a replacement for the B-17 and the B-24.

At this time, American bombers, although the most heavily armed in the world, were finding tough going against Luftwaffe fighters in the skies of Europe. A suitable escort fighter had not yet been found for the relatively short rang B-17, and so the army saw a need for far more effective defensive firepower for the new superbomber, which would not be able to count on friendly fighters to shoot it out with the enemy.

On the 20th of March, 1940, several months before a manufacturer for the projected bomber had been picked, a circular letter went out from Wright Field's Armament Lab. This letter expressed a requirement for an armament system to fit a four engined pressurized bomber with two .50 turrets and a twin .50 and single 20 m/m tail turret. Reliable functioning was required at speeds up to 450 mph at 40,000, all guns controlled from two or three sighting stations.

The circular went to GE, Bendix, Westinghouse, and Sperry, the latter's design being the winner. The Sperry system used retractable turrets with periscope sights and was installed on the first three prototypes. At this point, the Sperry design was abandoned and a

GE fire control system was adopted as standard and it remained through the life of the aircraft.

A backup plan to use manual turrets in case of failure of the remote system was carried out and installed on one B-29, but not used beyond that.

For the story of the B-29 in action, we turn to the words of one "who was there." Ex-TSgt Ray Pritchard, Jr., now postmaster in a city in Virginia, was CFC (Central fire control) gunner on B-29s with the 6th Bomb Grp (VH) and his thoughts on the Superfortress follow:

"The advent of the Boeing B-29 ushered in the first major change in aerial gunnery with its remote controlled, computer aligned, GE gunnery system. For the first time aerial gunners on a production-built operational bomber could aim and fire turrets of up to four caliber .50 machine guns that were as much as 60 feet away from him and furthermore he could fire as many as three of these turrets, two at a time. No longer did he have to figure windage, and lead or lag his target, nor worry about any other ballistics as all this was done for him by a marvelous little black box called a computer. Besides the back of the pilots seat, it was the only other thing in a B-29 protected by built-in armour plate. The gunner using his remote control electric sight was free to concentrate on aiming directly at his target by keeping it framed within his reticle of lighted dots and trying not to burn up his guns by firing short bursts. A formation of B-29s could throw out a deadly field of fire such as no attacking fighter pilot had ever had to face before.

"Before you accept this over-simplification as meaning that nearly any idiot could close his eyes and become an ace-gunner in a B-29, perhaps I better review a bit of the requirements and training required of a remote-control turret gunner, as his MOS (military occupational specialty) called him. Most B-29's had a gunnery crew consisting of a 'gunnery commander' known as a CFC, who occupied the top rear sighting blister just ahead of the upper rear turret. The upper forward plexiglass dome near the upper forward four-gun turret was actually an astrodome sighting station for the navigator, not a gunsight position. There were two side gunners known as left and right blister gunners, and a tail gunner who was isolated in his office except when the aircraft was not pressurized. The other sighting station was in the nose over the bombsight and primarily operated by the bombardier.

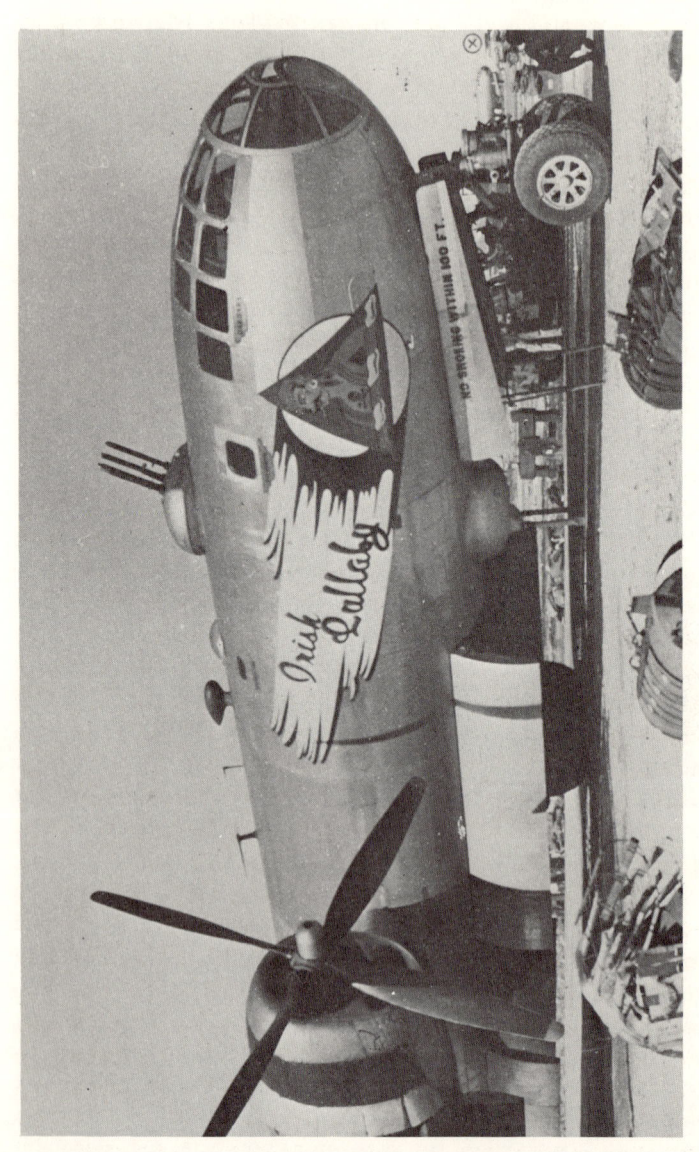

"Irish Lullaby" was a B-29 of the 6th Bomb Group (VH), seen here on Tinian in the Marianas in August of 1945. Both forward turrets are loaded, as indicated by vertical storage of guns, to prevent damage in case of accidental firing.
Ray Pritchard Photo

"All of these gunners went through the regular Air Force aerial gunner schools, plus the additional familiarization and light maintenance on the General Electric gunnery system. The CFC gunner who, according to the TO, was responsible for maintenance of the whole system in his B-29 also had to take a six weeks cram course on the electronic and mechanical design, maintenance, and operation of the system. This school operated on 24-hour basis, at Lowery Field, Denver. After this he went through the regular aerial gunnery school course of skeet ranges, firing from a pickup truck standing at a swivel mounted shot gun. In the air the prospective gunner flew in B-24's, in our case at Buckingham Field, Florida, firing both hand-held waist guns as well as all the turrets, at both water targets and towed sleeves. We even had a bit of firing at armoured P-39s and P-63s painted up like zebras, but we used a special frangible ammunition which shattered on impact, but with enough force to record the hit in the target aircraft. In addition to this we went on to fire the GE system mounted in rebuilt B-24's.

"Although very little else about the gunnery set-up on the B-29's resembled a mission in Europe based B-17's, the preflight arming procedure was pretty similar. Ground crew armorers actually did most of the maintenance of the guns themselves, and remote-control turret maintenance specialists kept the GE system tuned in top condition. In our 6th Bomb Group, the aircrew gunners usually went down to the flight line several hours before a mission and loaded the ammunition cans, checked and armed the guns in the turrets and generally preflighted the system. Although we had been taught that the guns and turrets could be freed of malfunctions in flight, it proved to be almost impossible, and jammed guns and inoperative turrets stayed that way until return to base.

"On August 8th, 1945 the 6th Bomb Group participated in the mission to Yawata with the Sasebo Naval Base and shipyards and the steel mills as the target. This turned out to be the last large B-29 mission of the war where any great fighter opposition from the Japanese was mounted against the 20th Air Force bombers. The events of the day should give a good picture of the B-29 remote-control GE gunnery system and its deadly effectiveness.

"Once airborne, the gunners on board the B-29's didn't have much to do on the long flight up to the mainland of Japan, normally about a seven hour flight across about 1700 miles of Pacific Ocean from our bases in the Marianna Islands, since no enemy opposition was normally expected until about 100 miles off the coast. The B-29 was such a tremendous improvement over anything previous, especially in creature comforts with its pressurized, air conditioned and heated crew compartments, that it was really more like a flight in an airliner of today as compared to the box car-like accommodations of the B-17's and the '24's, where at altitude over Europe even in summer, it was pure freezing misery to the gunners. At altitudes up to 35,000 feet and higher, we wore ordinary summer flight suits over T-shirts unencumbered by gloves or jackets, or even headgear, except for baseball caps. (Eat your hearts out, 8th AF gunners, we never told you till now!) Needless to say, this made for much greater combat readiness.

"The B-29's flew in formation over Japan by day and singly at night like the RAF bomber trains. As we were timed to pass over the target at high noon, we began endless circling in sight of Japan as the forming up by squadrons and groups began. Although this was the most vulnerable and dangerous time when fighter attacks could have played havoc, the desperate fuel situation of the Japanese Air Forces was very evident, since we did not receive even one pass by an enemy fighter while we were forming up off the coast. They preferred to save fuel and wait for their fighter controller to try and determine our targets before vectoring them in to intercept.

"It was not until just before we reached the forming up area that the gunners manned their gunsight positions. On signal from the pilot, we slipped into flak vests and steel infantry helmets and alerted ourselves and our gun positions. I was CFC, or top gunner, on our aircraft and climbed up into my plywood seat which was mounted on a round elevated platform, also plywood and thrust my head up into the little plastic bubble where my sight was located. As described elsewhere in the system description, each gunner was given his primary turret as I activated his sight by throwing the switches in the master gunnery control panel which activated the whole system. The tail gunner was back all alone in his separate pressurized position under the great rudder, sealed in by the airlock door. He still had two .50's, although his 20 m/m cannon had been permanently removed since the low-level Tokyo raids in March. They were never too effective in combination due to the different trajectories anyhow. The much more rapid fire of the .50's was preferred. Since the bombardier was primarily busy getting set up for his main job, the CFC gunners rigged the switches so that both upper turrets were tied into the CFC gunners sight. However, the bombardier could claim his upper forward turret on demand by pressing his primary control on the sight as well as having secondary control of the lower forward turret in case of frontal attacks. Both the bombardier and CFC had command of six .50's on demand. The side blister gunners had primary control of the lower forward and aft turrets and could swap them about so that either could use both, depending on which side was under attack. They could also take over the tail turret in the event of the tail gunner being knocked out. However, their sights were useless for dead aft aiming, except for blind spraying.

"With all the preliminaries out of the way and now completely formed up by squadrons and groups, the deadly armada began its track towards Yawata and thereby committed itself to fighter attack which was not long in coming. We in Myas' Dragon, #40 of the 39th Squadron, were on the left outside position of the V of Vs of 18 aircraft. The 12 o'clock to 6 o'clock area was of main concern to us in regards to possible fighter attack. We could hear the other aircraft begin to call in fighter sightings. A couple of twin-engined Nicks or Irvings had been flying along side us, about two miles out, for several minutes, radioing our course, altitude and speed. Every few miles a ground flak unit fired up white trailing phosphorus shells, visually marking our position as well. The whole Japanese Fighter Command was setting us up for the kill. We bore on towards our IP on Shimonosenki Straits under a cloudless summer sky, eyes and heads swiveling like mad. Our formations contained about 200 B-29s stacked up between 15,000 and 18,000 feet. The gunners in our particular group of 18 had command of 216 .50 caliber machine guns mounted in the finest turret system available, the possible hail of gunfire from such a formation was enough to make any fighter pilot in his right mind, a bit gun-shy. One twin-engined Nick started the ball rolling by diving straight down from the sun right through the middle of our formation so fast that no one even fired at him and he made no hits either. Another came barreling through head on with a combined closing speed of about 700 mph, as we were cruising at about 325 mph indicated. Once again no hits, but everyone had their adrenalin up by now and we knew we were going to get a workout — as predicted.

"We had been briefed that we would have an escort of P-51's and P-47N's from Iwo Jima, but so far, no show. Suddenly the navigator called out a P-47 at 10 o'clock high. I couldn't spot him at first and felt a little panicky because he kept calling him out and I still didn't see him — I was looking too far — finally saw him and the the great red meatballs on his side hit me right in the eye. 'That's a Frank,' I shouted, 'not a '47!' To give it its more formal name it was a Nakajima Ki.84 Hayate, was unpainted except for the honamaru (insignia), and was out only about 1,000 yards pulling up ahead for a pursuit curve attack. I barely had time to get him in my sight — we left them set for 37 foot wingspans — when he pulled up and over, coming in inverted with all his cannon winking red. I clamped down on the trigger, firing all six guns in the upper turrets. Right away he was hit and off flew his cowling with a black plume of smoke shooting back underneath. Everybody was banging away at him as he flashed below to complete his breakaway, still inverted. 'He's starting to spin,' yelled the tail gunner. Our brief moment of elation was ruined by the B-29 right off our right wing calling out that he was hit and feathering #3 engine, which caused him to drop behind right away. We were swearing because we thought the Frank had hit him after all. Tail gunner called out that the Frank was still spinning and trailing black smoke, but we went off and left him

Portrait of a WW-II air gunner, TSgt Raymond Pritchard, standing by the aft turret of B-29 "MYAS' DRAGON", of the 6th Bomb Group. The place is Iwo Jima and the time is 14 August, 1945, only moments after being told the war is over.   Ray Pritchard Photo

long before he reached the ground — no parachute though. The hit B-29 was dropping back fast and was down about 1,000 feet. Another pilot was almost demanding that he be released to drop back and cover him. He was refused by the Group Commander and told to tighten up and the whole formation ordered to increase speed to 330. We found out later that the cripple made it back to Okinawa, fighting all the way, and getting credit for shooting down five navy Georges. He took many hits but luckily no one was wounded on board — the aircraft never flew again.

"Our burning Frank didn't get him after all, it was a Nick that dove straight down from the sun getting through the middle of the formation so fast no one hit him, most didn't even see him.

"One hundred and seventy-five individual fighter attacks were reported on our formation, with no other B-29 losses that day.

"We were coming up on the IP fast now, and the flak began at this point and the fighters pulled off. A couple of cruisers in the harbor were really laying up the flak along with the area defense batteries. A formation off to our left at 7 o'clock had a carpet of black so thick under them you could walk on it — luckily it was 100 feet too low. By now, some two hundred and fifty B-29s were unloading 10 tons of 500 pounders apiece on Yawata at high noon. Some lunch hour!

"Radar Spook reported bomb bay doors closed and bomb bay clear. Back came the fighters as we roared up the straits. Where were those escorts? We had never had any before anyhow! Now five Tony's in echelon pulled up about 1500 yards off at 9 o'clock. They had a lot of black paint on them, meatballs on white. They just flew along looking us over for a few moments. We were really tensed up for this one. I thought they would turn in on the formation, instead only the leader tipped up and all hell broke loose — every plane on our side of the formation cut loose on him, and pieces were flying off him as he flashed under us diving away. Now came #2, same thing, but he broke away further out. The other three decided to linger out there awhile getting up nerve.

"What happened next shows just how effective the GE system was over the old power turrets and hand held guns, few of which had a range effective over 800 yards away. The three Tony's still sat out there in formation with us about 1200 yards away. As the next one looked like he might come in, I fired at him away out there. My tracers (which we used every 12 or so rounds, for scare) flashed right by his nose. He straightened up for a moment and then dove away to the left, quickly followed by #4. I'm sure I got hits on him away out there.

"Now #5 was out there all by himself. I don't blame him for thinking it over, but he concentrated too long. A P-47 dove on him from behind, firing as he came. The Tony pilot yanked the stick back into his stomach going into a tight loop with the '47 looping right outside him firing bursts all the way. They went around three times like this before the Tony stalled and fell off into a tight spiral, turning into a spin. That was the only fighter I ever saw shot down by another fighter, and I saw no other Thunderbolts. As we bored back down Shimonosenki Straits heading back towards the east coast of Honshu, and the long haul home, a large formation of P-51's flashed by towards Yawata, 5,000 feet below us — a little late fellows!

"In a few more minutes we cruised on by a sight I will never forget, the incredible desolation of Hiroshima. No one said a word on the air, or the intercom for five minutes at least. Our two hundred and fifty B-29's had not begun to do to Yawata what that one bomb dropped by the lone Enola Gay had done."

The last of the multi-turret bombers, the Convair B-36. This RB-36 of the 28th Bomb Wing shows its aft 20 m/m turrets in firing position. Usually retracted covered, the turrets were seldom seen or photographed.   Author's Collection

V
THE ARMED CHOPPER

Although, as stated in the introduction, no attempt will be made to cover bombs, or air-to-surface missiles in any detail, the general area of ground attack must be covered in discussing an increasingly important combat aircraft — the armed helicopter.

In the 30 years of development of the whirly bird, almost no attention has been given to any possibility of air-to-air combat involving rotary wing aircraft. Army tests have indicated that the most effective counter for a VTOL aircraft is another VTOL machine, but whether such situations will ever arise must await the future. As far as is known there has never been such a confrontation.

At least one such instance is known between a rotary wing aircraft and fixed wing fighters. This strange affair took place in July of 1943 over the coastline of England, near Dungeness, when two Fw 190's came upon an Avro-built Cierva autogiro of the RAF, which was flying on radar calibration duties. Although the 190's both attempted firing passes at the unarmed autogiro, its RAF pilot, a man named Norman Hill, was able to use the machine's maneuverability to avoid the attacks and successfully evaded to his home field as dusk closed in.

The entire trend of development in helicopter armament has been in the field of ASW (anti-submarine warfare), and in the strike role. This latter has been primarily close support of the foot soldier. The ASW helicopter is normally equipped with extensive search gear, air-to-surface missiles, and homing torpedos. No attempt will be made to delve into these interesting subjects.

The helicopter's military career began in the humanitarian role. Although the history of rotary wing aircraft goes back centuries, none with sufficient power or controllability appeared until the 1930s, and the first chopper to enter military service in any quantity did not do so until 1944. This was the Sikorsky R-4, and it rapidly began a lifesaving tradition which grows more incredible with each new rescue development.

Although some bomb-dropping experiments were tried with the R-4, no efforts to arm it were made. It was, in any case, too fragile and underpowered to mount a gun — a situation similar to the fixed wing aircraft of 30 years previous.

The helicopter was a seldom seen curiosity during WW-II, but by the early 1950s the fragile chopper had become a useful military vehicle. All of the U. S. services used it extensively in the Korean conflict, but its major use was in the rescue and logistics role — at which it excelled, and still does.

The most important rescue chopper in the early days of the Korean War was the Sikorsky R-5 (later H-5), and yet strangely enough, this machine was originally developed for ASW duties. In 1942 the British had devised the idea of operating radar equipped, and depth charge-armed helicopters off the decks of merchant ships for convoy protection. Sikorsky was asked to develop the idea and the R-5 was the result. With the end of WW-II, the scheme never

The experimental double-barrel Hughes 20 m/m cannon on a Sikorsky H-34 of Marine Helicopter Squadron One in 1959. Firing of the weapon tended to pull the helicopter off target. USMC Photo

reached fruition, but R-5's did carry, and release, depth charges during tests. Sikorsky also produced designs for a 20 m/m cannon installation, but it was never carried beyond the drawing board stage.

The first extensive use of the armed chopper seems to have been in the same area where this weapon is in such wide use by the U. S. today. About 1950, in what was the French Indo China, the French air force mounted a variety of weapons, including machine guns, rockets, and cannon, on Vertol H-21s, Sikorsky H-19s, and also the smaller types.

In the United States, armed helicopter development has been chiefly done by the U. S. Army at its Aviation Center at Fort Rucker, and by the USMC at Quantico, Virginia. In the Marine Corps, all experimental work on helicopters has been done by HMX-1 (Marine Experimental Helicopter Squadron #1), in conjunction with the Development Center, also located at Quantico.

HMX-1 was formed in December, 1947 before the Corps even had a helicopter and has been performing the same mission ever since. However, until recent years the helicopter was viewed by the Marines as an assault and logistics transport, and not a fighting aircraft.

A fire team of UH-1Ds rolls into firing run. Both of these Bell Hueys are armed with the M-6 armament subsystem, made up of four M-60 machine guns.   Bell Helicopter Photo

HMX-1 took its first step toward providing armament in the spring of 1950 when a rocket launcher mount was installed on the skid of a Bell HTL (Army H-13). Ammunition could not be obtained until August at which time the weapon was successfully fired in flight. There was, however, no effort to proceed any further with the idea.

Early in 1954 HMX-1 tried again with an interesting, but hair raising idea! The project was to drop napalm from a Sikorsky HRS (now H-19), but this type was always short on lifting power and could not handle the standard napalm containers. Someone (probably not one of the test crews), suggested that the napalm be put in glass one quart jars and dropped overboard by hand! Strangely enough it was done, a total of seven drops being made. However, the resulting fires were quite small, and the flight crews were totally unenthusiastic about a lap full of napalm in glass jars, and that was the end of that.

Although not a total success, the next attempt, in 1959, was much more practical. A new 20 m/m Hughes cannon was installed and tested on an H-34. However, a friend of the author's, and one of the officers involved in the tests, stated that there were numerous problems with the gun, and its recoil tended to pull the chopper off its target.

In the early 1960s, a directive from the Commandant indicated that no more work would be done on armed helicopters, and it was not until about 1964 that the Marines began an accelerated program of this nature, which continues to this day.

In the United States, the Army has been the most enthusiastic about the armed helicopter, and began to develop weapon systems for them in 1956 at Fort Rucker, and in March 1957 the Army Aviation School proposed the Sky Cavalry Platoon. This was a reconnaissance type force completely equipped with armed helicopters, and of course, is the origin of the famous 1st Air Cav. The first Army unit to take armed helicopter into combat was the Utility Tactical Transport Company, based on Okinawa, and deployed to Vietnam in mid-1962.

A whole series of weapon systems were developed and fitted to most Army choppers, and a few of the more important or interesting will be discussed briefly.

One of the most widely used is the M-6 Quad Machine Gun System. It consists of two flexible gun mounts, one on each side, and

One of the most versatile and widely used helicopter armament systems is the M-16, which consists of four M-60 machine guns and two 7-tube rocket launchers. The door gunner here is also armed with an M-60.

U. S. Army Photo

each mount carries two M-60C guns. Ammunition supply is over 6,000 rounds of 7.62 m/m. The guns have an up and down travel of 75 degrees, can be swung laterally over an arc of 82 degrees, or can be locked in position and fired as fixed guns. Although the M-6 can be used on almost any helicopter of sufficient size, its most common application is the Bell UH-1 Huey. The co-pilot is the gunner, although the pilot can fire the weapons.

The standard Army anti-tank helicopter is the UH-1D armed with six M-22 anti-tank missiles. This is the French-developed wire-guided SS-11. As it is launched it trails two lengths of wire which remain attached to the launcher. It is guided by a small wobble stick in front of the co-pilot who picks up the missile in an optical sight after launching, and guides it to its target. Its normal useful range is about 800 meters.

The famed Huey has carried an amazing variety of weapons, including the three-barreled version of the M-61 Vulvan 20 m/m cannon, the M-5 40 m/m grenade launcher, many different rocket packs, and of course, the revolving minigun.

Portrait of an air gunner of the '60s in action! This intrepid airman leans far out the door to bring his M-60 gun to bear on a target.

Bell Helicopter Photo

As this is written, the highest development of the armed chopper and the first to be designed for that purpose is the Bell Huey Cobra, the latest of which is the AH-1J, a twin engined machine for the Marines. Its built-in gun is the XM-197, mounted in a chin turret (remember the B-17?). This is a lightened 3-barrel version of the M-61 Gatling type 20 m/m cannon. The gunner occupies the front seat of the Cobra and is provided with 750 rounds of ammo — enough for about one minute of firing.

The Cobra which has proven the concept, however, is the earlier Army AH-1G, a single-engine machine which performs and sounds (to this writer, at least) much like a WW-II fighter plane. Its main armament is a chin turret (XM-28) which mounts both a 40 m/m grenade launcher and a 7.62 m/m minigun. In addition, the Cobra has stubby "wings" which mount a variety of rocket and weapon packs.

The Huey Cobras' combat record in Vietnam has been impres-

The most advanced of current in-service armed helicopters, the AH-1G, Huey Cobra. This one mounts a single minigun in its nose turret.
Bell Helicopter Photo

sive and the type will no doubt continue to be developed. In fact, in the entire field of the armed helicopter, a vast amount of research is being done by the services and by General Electric and Emerson, and other companies, and we can expect some exotic results in the coming years.

VI
FIGHTERS SINCE WORLD WAR TWO

The gas turbine engine (commonly referred to by the vague and not very correct term "jet") is one of the major milestones in aviation history. All of the major powers were flying aircraft powered by these new engines before the end of WW-II, but only the German, and a few British, were used in combat. With the end of that war, it seemed

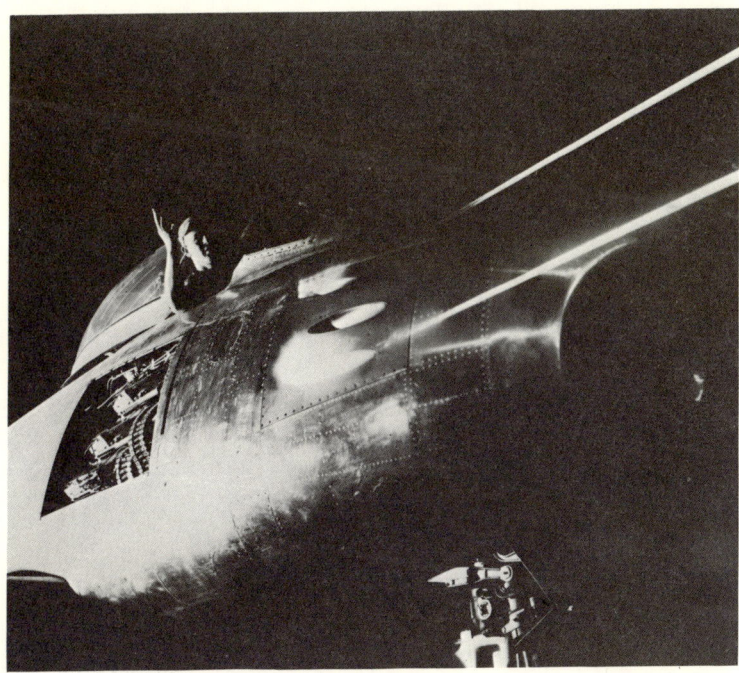

An F-86 Sabre of the 51st Fighter Wing undergoing gun firing tests in Korea, in September of 1952. Apparently only two of the six M3 Brownings are firing.   Air Force Photo

obvious that fighters from that time on, would employ no more piston engines.

The new generation of fighters did not immediately provide much new in armament. In the U. S. the F-80, F-84, and the F-86 were the first of the new generation of jet fighters, and their firepower depended on the still-standard six .50 Brownings, grouped together in the nose.

When Communist aggression replaced Japanese aggression in the Far East in 1950, with the attack on South Korea, the United States was again involved in a shooting war. American fighters involved in this nasty little war were the above mentioned types, plus the navy F9F, and a great many of those two stalwarts of WW-II, the F4U Corsair and the P-51 Mustang. These half dozen types exhibited little new in the armament field except for the radar gunsight on the F-86, which did the bulk of the air fighting.

Although the first generation of jet fighters had retained the quarter-century old .50 Browning, a new development had taken place about this same time, on a fighter with a specialized mission — the all weather fighter. These were typified by the F-89, the F-94 and the F-86D, all turbine powered and with extensive radar to fit their dirty weather mission. In their final versions, all of these mounted a new weapon — the rocket propelled airborne interception missile (AIM), and there was not a gun among them.

Of course, the rocket missile was not really a new weapon, its first use in combat going back to the 1914-18 war. These were the LePrieur electrically-fired rockets, mounted on the interplane struts of Nieuport Scouts, and used with some success against German captive observation balloons.

During WW-II, the RP (rocket projectile) became an important Allied weapon for use against ground and maritime targets. Its only use in air-to-air combat was by the Luftwaffe, which was desperately trying a wide variety of weapons in their attempts to stop the heavy bombers of the AAF and the RAF.

By the late 1940s, the rocket art had advanced to the point where engineers felt it was ready to be the sole armament on all weather fighters. The missiles of these early fighters were all of the unguided type. The North American F-86D was typical of that era, although it differed from the others in being a single seater.

The "Sabre Dog" was armed with 24 of the folding fin navy-developed 2.75 "Mighty Mouse" rockets. They were housed in a re-

A well kept F-86 of the Tennessee ANG. The "Sabre Dog" had no guns, but was armed with "Mighty Mouse" rockets carried in a retractable tray just behind the nose wheel door. Author's Photo

tractable launcher and were fired in groups (or in salvo) in response to signals from the Hughes E-4 fire control system. The "Mighty Mouse" had a warhead weighing 7.55 pounds and a range of about 4500 yards.

Vestiges of the WW-II K-14 gunsight can be seen in the Hughes E-4 fire control, since one of its major components was a computer. Range information for the computer was fed in by the AN/APG 37 radar dish antenna in the nose, whose maximum range was about 30 miles.

When a blip appeared on the scope the radar "locked in" to the computer which determined the proper course to fly. This was accomplished by the pilot by keeping a dot in the center of the scope. The pilot also selected the number of rockets to fire (6, 12, or salvo), and depressed the firing switch. However, this action did not fire the rockets. The computer completed the firing circuit when F-86 and target were in the proper positions. The rocket pack then extended, fired all rockets (if salvo had been selected) and returned to its retracted position, all in less then 5 seconds! The Sabre-Dog lived out its operational life without ever engaging a real target.

One of the earliest and most successful of all guided air-to-air missiles is the Sidewinder, which was conceived at the U. S. Naval Ordnance Test Station at China Lake, California in the mid 1950s. It was further developed and built in quantity by the Philco Corporation, under the designation AIM-9. It is nine feet long, weighs 155 pounds, is powered by a solid fuel rocket engine, and is guided by an infra-red sensor in the nose. It is, therefore, a heat-seeking missile and will lock on to heat emitted from a target aircraft. One of the current versions, the Sidewinder 9C, also has an interchangeable radar guidance head.

Although developed by and for the USN, its simplicity and effectiveness caused the USAF to adopt it in 1957. It is still in wide use by both services, as well as many other countries, at the beginning of the 1970s.

It was in fact, the first air-to-air guided missile to destroy an enemy aircraft in combat, when Chinese Nationalists pilots, flying F-86F's, shot down several communist MIG-15's over the Straits of Formosa in September 1958.

Another widely used air-to-air missile which entered service in the late 1950s, and remained part of U. S. fighter armament during the decade of the 1960s, is the unguided Genie, used on the F-101B, the F-106, and the elderly F-89. Interestingly enough, this latter fighter, although totally obsolete, was still in service with ANG squadrons at this writing.

Still an important weapon in the USAF inventory is the Hughes Falcon, which forms the main armament of the F-102 and the F-106, and is also adapted to the F-4D. The Falcon in its many variations has a velocity ranging from Mach 2 to Mach 6, and a range beyond five miles. In its AIM-47A version it carries a nuclear warhead, but most models use a conventional warhead. Its guidance system can be infra-red homing or radar.

The AIM gained considerably in importance during the 1950s and 60s, and there appeared to be a trend away from guns. Nevertheless the cannon remained in varying degrees throughout the world, in a wide variety of aircraft. When North American designed the F-100 Super Sabre as the successor of the F-86, the old reliable M-3 Browning was not part of its armament. Although the F-86/caliber .50 combination had scored heavily in Korea against communist fighters, there was at that time much agitation for bigger guns, and in the F-100 these were provided in the form of four M-39E 20 m/m cannon. The M-39 in its early stages, was developed by the Illinois Institute of Technology, Ford Motor Company taking over in 1950. Near the end of the Korean war, several F-86F's were shipped to Korea armed with M-39s, where they shot down several MIG's before the end of hostilities. The Pontiac Division of General Motors then was awarded contracts for large scale production of the wea-

Hawker Hunters of 208 Squadron, RAF, seen here at Sharjah on the Persian Gulf in August, 1966. Powder smoke around the gun ports show that the 30 m/m Aden cannon have been recently fired.
Photo by Flt. Lt. Russell-Smith, RAF

pon, and it is still in service with the USAF at this writing.

The M-39 undoubtedly owes its origin to the German Mauser MG-213 revolver cannon, but there are significant differences. Both are gas operated, belt-fed, firing electrically-detonated ammunition, and both use the five-pound revolving cylinder. In the Mauser the cylinder indexed with the barrel at the 12 o'clock position, while the M-39 cylinder and barrel index at the six o'clock position when in battery. The M-39 fires at about 1600 rounds per minute, and the effective range is about 1200 yards. In the F-100 each gun is provided with 275 rounds per gun, or about 10 seconds of firing time.

There was one other important aircraft gun in the western world which owed its origin to the Mauser, and this is the British Aden gun used in the Hawker Hunter and others. Unlike the M-39, the Aden (Armament Development Enfield) is in 30 m/m caliber.

By the end of WW-II, the USN had begun a changeover from the .50 Browning to the 20 m/m cannon, the F4U-4B being the first important fighter aircraft to make the change. The gun was again the familiar Hispano Suiza, known in U. S. services as the AN-M2. Through many modifications and variation, the Hisso remained the standard USN aircraft gun through the years and armed the F-8 Crusader and the Douglas A-4 Skyhawk.

By far the most important guns in the U. S. aircraft armament inventory are the General Electric revolving barrel weapons, all of which are of the Gatling type. The name of course, is that of Dr. Richard Gatling who first successfully produced a multiple revolving-barrel rapid-fire gun in the 1860s. Gatling's weapon was not a true machine gun because the operating and firing mechanism was activated by a hand crank, and its rate of fire depended on how fast the crank was turned.

General Electric's guns follow the same principle in that most of them are powered by an outside source, either electrically or hydraulically. The revolving-barrel gun (six barrels are standard, with one three-barrel gun in production) presents several advantages, primarily a very high rate of fire — up to 10,000 rounds per minute for the 5.56 m/m gun — with reduced barrel erosion, and increased gun life. With an externally-driven gun, there is little problem with dud cartridges, they are simply removed from the firing chambers in the normal cycle and discarded with the empty cases.

Although these guns have been built in calibers from .223 (5.56 m/m) to 30 m/m, the most widely used are the famous M61 Vulcan in 20 m/m, and the GAU-2B/A minigun in 7.62 m/m. The M61 is the standard weapon on the F-104 and F-105, while the newer M61A1 is "built in" on the F-4E Phantom and the new A-7D & E. The rate of fire is variable up to 6,000 rounds per minute. A late development of the basic Vulcan is the XM-130 (GAU-4) which is a self-powered gun, driven by the energy of its own powder gases, instead of the external power of the M61.

Another development of recent years is the linkless feed system which delivers cartridges from the ammunition drum to the gun and returns empties to a storage space in the drum. The familiar old ammunition belt links are eliminated completely from this system.

Dr. Gatling's multiple barrel principle of a century ago, brought up to date by General Electric, will apparently continue to be the only important gun in U. S. built combat aircraft for some time to come. Besides its aircraft application, a new air defense system has been built around the 20 m/m gun for the U. S. Army, and the 7.62 minigun is increasingly found on pintle (post) mounts on helicopters, water craft, and land vehicles.

The McDonnell-Douglas F-4, which is normally armed with the radar homing Mach 3 Raytheon AIM-7 Sparrow III, is the most important fighter in the western world, and will probably remain so throughout the early 1970s.

When the F-4 was designed in the mid-1950s, the "missile instead of guns" theory won out, and as a result the F-4 was designed around four Raytheon Sparrows mounted in recessed belly positions.

Sidewinder! The first of the heat-seeking air-to-air missiles, and still in wide usage today.
Philco-Ford Photo

In addition, two other Sparrows or four Sidewinders could be accommodated on wing pylons. There were no guns at all.

Although designed to a naval requirement, the F-4 Phantom was obviously superior to anything in USAF service, and the Air Force ordered the aircraft as the F-4C, which retained the same basic armament.

Even though the air-to-air guided missile was assuming dominance in the years between Korea and Vietnam, there were many USN and USAF fighter pilots who were skeptical of the situation and felt decidedly naked without a built-in gun.

In mid-1965 the F-4 embarked on its combat career in the skies of North Vietnam, where its primary mission was escort for the bomb-laden Republic F-105 "Thuds." It rapidly became apparent that the theorists had been wrong and the skeptical fighter pilots had been right — an inbuilt gun was badly needed because of severe limitations in missile performance in a dogfight situation.

In the many air combats over North Vietnam, USAF and Navy fighter crews were on the winning side of the ledger against communist MIG 17's and 21, but only to a ratio of about 2 to 1, while 15 years before, in Korea, the ratio had been about 10 to 1.

Speaking at the American Fighter Aces Association meeting in 1968, Colonel Robin Olds described several encounters in which he failed to destroy an enemy aircraft because of the lack of a cannon. Olds shot down four MIGs in Vietnam and remains the highest scoring American pilot of that conflict, although he feels that he would have done considerably better if a cannon had been available.

At the request of the Air Force, GE took immediate steps to develop a pod-mounted M61 Vulcan, mounted on external racks, and these were used with some success before President Johnson ordered an end to air attacks over the North.

The lesson had been clear enough and the USAF passed the word to McDonnell that it wanted a built-in gun. The result was the F-4E, armed with a nose-mounted M61A1 cannon.

Curiously enough, although navy pilots were equally eager for a built-in gun, the USN has not taken any steps to provide one in its F-4's, and RAF Phantoms are also rigged only for the pod mounted weapon.

However, the trend away from aircraft guns appears to be solidly reversed, and the new USAF fighter, the F-15, will mount a gun of 25 or 30 m/m with variable rates of fire and using caseless ammunition. Probably two different AIMs will complete the F-15's armament system.

VII
VIETNAM

During the second half of the 1960s, the United States became heavily involved in one of its most tragic wars. Any sane man recognizes that all wars are filled with tragedy, but the Vietnam War was especially so because of the confusion generated among the American people (both innocently and intentionally) until the original purpose or cause — which seems to have been a just one, became muddied beyond recognition.

Regardless of the damaging consequences of the Vietnam War on the unity of American People, it provided many technically and historically-interesting developments.

Besides the massive use of heavy bombers in the tactical role, and that of fighters in both tactical and strategic missions, many ideas in the aircraft armament field that had been abandoned as much as half a century ago, were to reappear. Probably the oldest of these ideas was the use of a standard infantry rifle, handled and fired by the pilot of a single engine "scout" aircraft. This was, of course, the M16 rifle carried by the FAC (Forward Air Controller) in his aged Cessna O-1.

Another anachronism was the hand-held free-firing rifle-caliber machine gun. Abandoned 20 years before, it was brought up to date in the form of an M-60 machine gun in the doorway of a Huey (and other) helicopters. The intrepid gunners who often leaned far out the doorway to bring their guns to bear on a target, would have been amused at their resemblance to the first air gunners over France in 1914.

Many "antique" aircraft came back for another war, and one of the most important was the Douglas A-1, the "Able Dog" of Navy fame. Destined for further service with the USAF after Navy phase-out, the "Spad's" built-in armament of four 20 m/m cannon was used almost entirely in the ground support role, along with a heavy

McDonnell F-4B's of Marine Fighter Squadron 115, at DaNang, South Vietnam in May of 1966. The Phantom remains the most important fighter aircraft in the western world. In this version there is no built-in gun armament.   Marine Corps Photo

Representative of General Electric's family of revolving-barrel Gatling-type guns is this 7.62 m/m minigun — the GUA-2B/A. pintle-mounted here on a Bell UH-1F.   Author's Photo

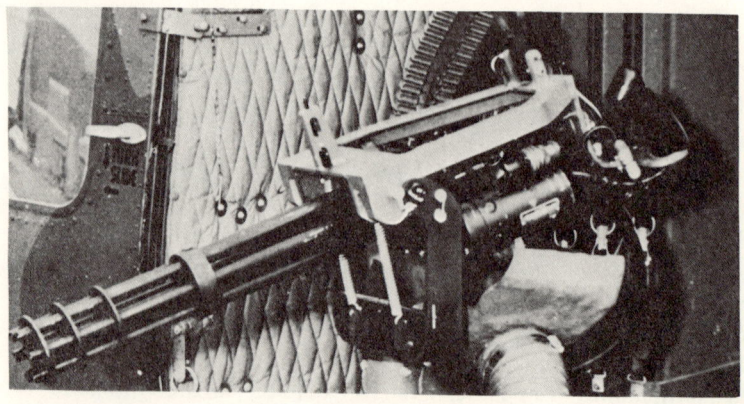

load of other assorted ordnance. Nevertheless, during the early years of the war Navy pilots managed to shoot down several inept or overconfident communist pilots in jet fighters of the MIG 17 type.

The reader who is familiar with combat in Vietnam will also be aware of at least one major difference between the above cited examples and their counterparts of earlier years. In previous applications, the hand-held rifles and machine guns were meant for use (hopefully) against other aircraft. As used in Southeast Asia in the 1960s, this firepower was applied only to ground targets.

We will bring our short story of aircraft armament to a close with another strange development of the Vietnam war, which is, an interesting part of that story.

The Douglas C-47, the "Goony Bird," is quite possibly the most famous airplane ever built, and has probably spread its tapered wings over more areas of the earth for a longer period of time then any other flying machine in history. First flown in the mid-1930s, the DC-3 (or C-47, C-53, Skytrain, Dakota, and many other names) has plodded on into the '70s in diminishing numbers but still with no retirement in sight.

Until Vietnam however, the C-47 had spent her years in relatively peaceful pursuits. True, she had been shot at over the years many times, but seldom had she ever had the ability to shoot back. In 1965, however, after a quarter of a century of world-wide service, the "Gooney" became a fighter.

The idea apparently had its origin in a unique technique used to lower light supplies and mail from a transport aircraft. A container on the end of a rope was lowered from the cargo door, and as long as the aircraft orbited in a small circle the container tended to hang in the same place.

Once the idea had been proposed, experiments were tried in the field, and USAF Systems Command went to work to develop the idea.

Early attempts by the 1st Air Commando Squadron, used a varying numbers of caliber .30 machine guns mounted in the doorway and the left windows. These were soon replaced by modification kits using three GE GAV-2B/1 7.62 m/m miniguns.

An immediate success, more C-47's were withdrawn from storage at Davis-Montham AFB, and from ANG units, modified in Florida, armed at Forbes AFB, Kansas, and flown out to the combat zone. Originally designated FC-47 (fighter cargo), it was soon

The muzzle of the M-61 Vulcan cannon can be seen just behind the radome of this Republic F-105 of the 388th Tactical Fighter Wing in Thailand, 1967.   Air Force Photo

One of the longest-lived of combat aircraft, the "Able Dog" of Navy fame, now designated A-1, is seen here in the colorful markings of the Vietnam Air Force.   Tom Hansen Photo

changed to AC-47 (Attack cargo), and the first flight of 20, belonging to the 4th Air Commando Squadron, went out to Vietnam in November, 1965.

On the AC-47, the pilot is also the gunner, using a lateral sight in the left window. The aircraft must be kept in a 30-degree bank at 125 knots airspeed, usually at about 3,000 feet altitude. The guns are fixed on their mounts with a 12-degree depression. Using these techniques, a very heavy concentration of fire can be supplied to a very small area. Night operations are more common then day, the target being illuminated by flares, either from the AC-47 or another flare-dropping aircraft.

Although the 3,000-foot altitude keeps the aircraft above the effective range of most small arms fire, about half a dozen have been lost in action.

As this is written (early 1970) the AC-47 has been replaced in USAF service by more modern machines, and hopefully the "Gooney Bird" will fight no more, but will return to being a nostalgic sight for many more years in a world of DC-8s and Boeing 747s.

In case the reader is wondering which "modern" aircraft replaced the C-47, it was another old timer making a comeback — the Fairchild C-119, or "Dollar-Nineteen" as she is widely known. Modified into a highly efficient attack aircraft, the new names are "Shadow" and "Stinger." (The AC-47 was often called "Spooky")

The latest of these, the AC-119K is armed with four miniguns

AC-47 firing at ground target north of Pleiku, January, 1967. Armament was three 7.62 m/m miniguns.   Air Force Photo

An Air Force F-100 Supersabre over South Vietnam's lower Mekong Delta, April, 1966. Armament was four M-39 20 m/m cannon.

Air Force Photo

and two M61 Vulcan cannon. However, the guns themselves are not the whole story with the 1970 version of the 119, as its big cargo compartment is jammed with very advanced navigation equipment, target sensing and tracking gear, a target illuminator, and automatic flare dispensers.

The journey from College Park in 1912 into the 1970s, has been a long one. Even so, the mission is still the same: to provide sufficiently-strong air arms to protect this country from its external enemies.